Benedict —

with my love

Dad

October 15ᵗʰ 1992

ERIC GILL & DAVID JONES
AT CAPEL-Y-FFIN

ERIC GILL & DAVID JONES AT CAPEL-Y-FFIN

Jonathan Miles

Border Lines Series Editor
John Powell Ward

SEREN BOOKS

for Derek Shiel

SEREN BOOKS is the book imprint of
Poetry Wales Press Ltd
Andmar House, Tondu Road,
Bridgend, Mid Glamorgan

The Text © Jonathan Miles, 1992
The Series Preface © John Powell Ward, 1992

British Library Cataloguing in Publication Data

Miles, Jonathan, *1952-*
Eric Gill and David Jones at Capel-y-ffin
(Border Lines series)
I. Title II. Series
709.22

ISBN 1-85411-051-9
ISBN 1-85411-052-7 pbk

*The publisher acknowledges the financial assistance of the
Welsh Arts Council*

Cover photograph taken by Stuart Smith

Printed in 10.5 point Plantin
by The Cromwell Press Ltd, Melksham

Contents

List of Illustrations

Series Preface

The Border country is that region between England and Wales which is upland and lowland, both and neither. Centuries ago kings and barons fought over these Marches without their national allegiance ever being settled. In our own time, referring to his own childhood, that eminent borderman Raymond Williams once said: "We talked of 'the English' who were not us, and 'the Welsh' who were not us." It is beautiful, gentle, intriguing, and often surprising. It displays majestic landscapes, which show a lot, and hide some more. People now walk it, poke into its cathedrals and bookshops, fly over or hang-glide from its mountains, yet its mystery remains.

In cultural terms the region is as fertile as (in parts) its agriculture and soil. The continued success of the Three Choirs Festival and the growth of the border town of Hay as a centre of the secondhand book trade have both attracted international recognition. The present series of introductory books is offered in the light of such events. Writers as diverse as Mary Webb, Raymond Williams and Wilfred Owen are seen in the special light — perhaps that cloudy, golden twilight so characteristic of the region — of their origin in this area or association with it. There are titles too, though fewer, on musicians and painters. The Gloucestershire composers such as Samuel Sebastian Wesley, and painters like David Jones, bear an imprint of border woods, rivers, villages and hills.

How wide is the border? Two, five or fifteen miles each side of the boundary; it depends on your perspective, on the placing of the nearest towns, on the terrain itself, and on history. In the time of Offa and after, Hereford itself was a frontier town, and Welsh was spoken there even in the nineteenth century. True border folk traditionally did not recognize those from even a few

miles away. Today, with greater mobility, the crossing of boundaries is easier, whether for education, marriage, art or leisure.
For myself, who spent some childhood years in Herefordshire
and much of the past ten crossing between England and Wales
once a week, I can only say that as you approach the border you
feel it. Suddenly you are in that finally elusive terrain, looking
from a bare height down on to a plain, or from the lower land up
to a gap in the hills, and you want to explore it, maybe not to
return.

This elusiveness pertains to the writers and artists too. Did the
urbane Elizabeth Barrett Browning, living just outside Ledbury
till her late twenties, have a border upbringing? Are the 'English
pastoral' composers, with names like Parry, Howells, and
Vaughan Williams, English, or are they indeed Welsh? One wonders whether border country is now suddenly found on the English side of the Severn Bridge, and how far even John Milton's
Comus, famous for its first production in Ludlow Castle, is in any
sense such a work. Then there is the fascinating Uxbridge-born
Peggy Eileen Whistler, transposed in the 1930s into Margiad
Evans to write her visionary novels set near her adored Ross-on-
Wye and which today still retain a magical charm. Further north:
could Barbara Pym, born and raised in Oswestry, even remotely
be called a border writer? Most people would say that the poet
A.E.Housman was far more so, yet he hardly ever visited the
county after which his chief book of poems, *A Shropshire Lad,* is
named. Further north still: there is the village of Chirk on the
boundary itself, where R.S.Thomas had his first curacy; there is
Gladstone's Hawarden library, just outside Chester and actually
into Clwyd in Wales itself; there is intriguingly the Wirral town
of Birkenhead, where Wilfred Owen spent his adolescence and
where his fellow war poet the Welsh Eisteddfod winner Hedd
Wynn was awarded his Chair — posthumously.

On the Welsh side the names are different. The mystic Ann
Griffiths; the metaphysical poet Henry Vaughan; the astonishing
nineteenth century symbolist novelist Arthur Machen (in Linda
Dowling's phrase, "Pater's prose as registered by Wilde"); and the
remarkable Thomas Olivers of Gregynog, author of the well-
known hymn 'Lo he comes with clouds descending'. Those descending clouds...; in border country the scene hangs overhead,
and it is easy to indulge in inaccuracies. Most significant perhaps

is the difference to the two peoples on either side. From England, the border meant the enticement of emptiness, a strange unpopulated land, going up and up into the hills. From Wales, the border meant the road to London, to the university, or to employment, whether by droving sheep, or later to the industries of Birmingham and Liverpool. It also meant the enemy, since borders and boundaries are necessarily political. Much is shared — yet different languages are spoken, in more than one sense.

With certain notable exceptions, the books in this series are short introductory studies of one person's work or some aspect of it. There are no footnotes or indexes. The bibliography lists main sources referred to in the text, and sometimes others, for anyone who would like to pursue the topic further. The authors reflect the diversity of their subjects. They are specialists or academics; critics or biographers; poets or musicians themselves; or ordinary people with however an established reputation of writing imaginatively and directly about what moves them. They are of various ages, both sexes, Welsh and English, border people themselves or from further afield.

The present book is the first account devoted exclusively to the four-year period in which Eric Gill and David Jones collaborated in the artist's community set up by Gill at Capel-y-Ffin in the Black Mountains in the nineteen twenties. Jonathan Miles's extensive and original research fills out for a short vital period the intense feelings of two creative and religiously obsessive people in a remote mountainous place; one middle-aged, domineering, sexually extreme even by modern standards; the other younger, far more self-effacing, shell-shocked by the First World War, yet with a prodigious talent which was to make him probably the leading British poet-painter since William Blake and earlier. Miles's familiarity with all the foundational aspects of the matter — Catholic mediaeval theology, art criticism, typography, evidence of diaries and letters — lead to this multilayered insight into a way of life, one which was itself a window on creative practice with its entire human underpinnings. Jonathan Miles has already published a book and several articles on the work of David Jones.

John Powell Ward

"We hired a lorry at Pandy, twelve miles away (the nearest station at which the pony could be detrained) and arrived at Capel about tea time in a typical steady Welsh downpour. But I have not said anything about our destination.... I should need a separate book to do it properly."

Eric Gill, *Autobiography*

1. Foreword

For Eric Gill, who felt that he had his back to the wall in his fight against the modern industrial way of life, Capel-y-ffin seemed to offer an ideal refuge:

> "I was in S. Wales...last week looking at a farm. We may buy it! 14m. from Abergavenny. Capel-y-ffin's the name and just describes it. 2000 feet of mountain wall on both sides & to north of it - no outlet but to the South. 4m. N. of Llanthony Abbey Ruins. Benedictine monastery 400 yards away — Bd. Sacrament & Dy Mass........Good land — fair price... Sheep run on mountains & stone galore, both for carving & building, *no extra charge*. 10 miles to Ry. Station. Postman on horse-back once a day. Doctor on horseback, from Hay, once a week. Any complaints?' (LET 175)

Gill did not buy the farm in question but he was attracted by the isolation of the Anglo-Welsh border country.

At the time of this visit to Capel-y-ffin Gill was living and working on Ditchling Common in Surrey in a Catholic artistic community. However, the situation at Ditchling had become too public and the communal organization was proving increasingly unsatisfactory to Gill who was reaching the stage of what he later described as his "spiritual puberty" (AUT 223); he was quite simply feeling the need to be the unquestioned master. Isolation in the border uplands would enable Gill to live away from prying eyes and challenging egos.

Now a border line is where two differences meet, often causing tension. It is a line of demarcation, often arbitrarily or artificially determined, which, once registered, can assume incredible importance. Seen from either side it constitutes a boundary, an edge, it provokes the necessity to admit otherness. The two great talents who worked at Capel-y-ffin, David Jones and Eric Gill, both in their different ways found themselves, at least metaphorically or notionally, over some sort of border and in a strange land.

ERIC GILL & DAVID JONES AT CAPEL-Y-FFIN

To be a Catholic in England in the early twentieth century was to be part of an esoteric minority. To be a Catholic who participated in an arts and crafts type experiment in communal living and who was known to have erotic preoccupations that disturbed his ecclesiastical supporters was to be a man on the borders of, or even beyond, respectability. So Gill went across an actual border into an almost inaccessible Welsh valley in order to secure a necessary freedom. The fact that it was the Anglo-Welsh border that he actually crossed was of little significance to Gill, rather it was the geophysically daunting position of Capel that made its appeal; it was surrounded by mountain walls, the iniquitous industrialized world could be kept out and domestic idiosyncrasies could escape scrutiny. Furthermore, the isolation of Capel necessitated frequent sallies into the outside world for work and play; Gill, like an intermittent cenobite, could come down from his mountain hideout and denounce (whilst also enjoying) the neurotic civilization that spread at his feet.

It was the complexity of Gill's personality that kept him hopping back and forth across this border which separated privacy and publicity, blessed wilderness and infernal civilization. He needed these antagonisms for the tenor of his writing is clearly reactionary. Not being a particularly patient or subtle thinker he required an enemy to galvanize his ideas. And, what is more, if we look at the inconsistencies in Gill's thinking and character and at his attempts to reconcile what appeared to be mutually exclusive, then the image of a border line is appropriate. For while a border separates differing identities it is in itself too sharp and too sudden a demarcation to be totally respectable; border lands are contested areas and on either side the influence of the other is felt. It is within this tension, where grey areas deny the facility of the unreal categories of black and white, that the drama of Eric Gill is located.

For David Jones, the actual tension between England and Wales which is so evident among the protagonists of *In Parenthesis* (his semi-autobiographical celebration of life in the trenches) is of supreme importance. While, as René Hague notes, the area around Capel was in the 1920s very much an anglicized border land with no Welsh spoken, and while David Jones hardly talked to the people round about, finding them 'strange and frightening" (DG 33), the landscape itself had a profound and

14

immediate effect on his painting. And things observed in Wales continued to appear in his work even decades later. The wattle fence, for example, in *Y Cyfarchiad I Fair*, one of Jones's last drawings and watercolours made in 1963, had been observed and sketched nearly forty years earlier at Capel; in the intervening period Jones was much preoccupied with such questions as the religious significance for the early Welsh of such a *bangor* or wattled enclosure.

The terrain surrounding Capel also gave a tangible quality to Jones's later writing which treated Wales largely as an imagined construct, by providing actually observed images that readily expressed or characterized a poetic dispensation. Jones found in the landscape and atmosphere of this *'Gwlad y Hûd'* (RQ 17) or 'Land of Enchantment', telling images of the transformative possibilities of the creative mode:

> Even at the confines
> > where this is that, that, perhaps was this,
> even there, where is the moving wall of mist where
> was the pillared hall. (RQ 14)

In Welsh mythology the passage from natural to supernatural frequently occurs, if not in caves, then at some boundary such as a stream or at the edge of water, and consequently Jones looked upon the boundary or border as a place of transition. Certainly in the *tir y blaenau*, the border uplands about Capel-y-ffin, Jones himself experienced the transition to creative maturity.

As we can apply the idea of the tensions of a border area to Gill's life, so we can see how the idea of polarization which is associated with a line of division or border becomes the underlying principle of structuring in David Jones's later poetry: London/Wales, Rome/Wales, civilization/culture, technocracy/locality. Such dichotomies underpin both the poetry and some of Jones's later mythological drawings and watercolours.

In differing ways both men, even the "absolutely, colossally English" Eric Gill (DJ BBC HRC), shared the common destiny of spending their lives on the perimeter of English society. Both men felt uncomfortable in the industrialized, commercialized world; both experienced emotional difficulties; both espoused an essentially exotic religion; both experienced anxieties about class;

both enjoyed community life and yet both felt the need of a life apart. Although Wales itself proved, in the end, to be practically difficult, Robert Gibbings, in a letter to Eric Gill, wittily and poignantly expressed the suitability of such backwaters for people at odds with English norms:

> If you ever leave Wales lets all go to Ireland there's no living there for such as us but even the thorn tree in the hedge gets its chance there so why shouldn't we...(WAC).

2. So Far

In January 1924 Eric Gill went to the Benedictine monastery on Caldey Island to discuss the possibility of the transfer of the Ditchling community to the Black Mountains. The idea had been under consideration for some time; Gill had written to the Prior of Caldey in February of the previous year discussing terms and requirements. From Caldey Gill travelled to Llanthony to get an impression of the environment; he found both his journey and the place itself "marvelous" (D 14.1.24). Two months later, in mid-March, he returned and collected a sample of Capel-y-ffin stone, which, a few days later back at Ditchling, he was busy carving. As a possible refuge from the increasingly notorious Ditchling the isolation of Capel made an immediate appeal.

Many years before, in 1188 to be exact, Gerald du Barri had discovered qualities in the Ewyas Valley that would prove attractive to men like Gill. He found it "most suited to the life of contemplation" and also noted that it would be "able...to supply its own wants" (JW 98). Some years prior to Gerald the valley had exerted a spellbinding effect on William de Lacy, a Norman Marcher Lord warring with the Welsh during the reign of Henry I. This Lord of Hereford found God in the valley and vowing to spend the rest of his life in seclusion and contemplation called himself William the Anchorite. In 1103 he was joined by Henry's chaplain Ernisius, and they created a community under the patronage of Queen Maud, building and finishing Llanthony Priory by 1115 (ODP 119). Just over four centuries later this Priory suffered at the greedy hands of Henry VIII and fell into decay. However, in the second half of the nineteenth century the Ewyas valley attracted yet another soul in search of the ideal place to serve the Lord in solitude. In November 1869 Joseph Leycester Lyne arrived with a postulant and, undaunted by the testing winter climate, laid in the spring of 1870 the corner-stone of a new monastery four miles to the north-west of Llanthony, just outside Capel-y-ffin. This monastery was designed by a notable Victorian architect, Charles Buckeridge, in the popular style known as Gothic Revival. Although Lyne, or Fr. Ignatius as he came to be known, was an able fund-raiser, he never received support from the Anglican authorities and his experiment failed, not only because of the remoteness of the place and because of his own frequent absences but also because of the lack of such vital support. At his death he wished the monastery to pass into the hands of Catholics, but because insufficient legal arrangements were made the monastery became a dependency of the Anglican Benedictine community on Caldey Island off Tenby on the coast of Pembrokeshire. These Benedictines had their own troubles with the Anglican authorities and, in 1913, gained admission to the Roman Catholic Church. Mass was celebrated at Capel-y-ffin by a Roman Catholic priest for the first time on 13 July of that year and until 1916 the Caldey monks visited the Black Mountains for their holidays. However, for the eight years before Gill began to rent the property, because of wartime difficulties and subsequent disrepair, the monastery remained empty.

So when Gill arrived "about midnight in deep snow" having driven "slowly and dangerously up a narrow and very rough mountain lane" the monastery that he found was "beginning to go to ruin". The buildings, organized around a central garth in "outwardly miserable but inwardly excellent Victorian sham Gothic" were, Gill thought, "just the thing for a small community" (AUT 217).

To the east of the monastery, the brownstone Hatteral Ridge (*Mynydd Gadair*) forms the border between England and Wales and along the top of this impressive ridge runs Offa's Dyke Path. Gerald du Barri described the Ewyas valley as being "shut in on all sides by a circle of lofty mountains", noting that it "is no more than three arrow-shots in width" (JW 96). Thorn, birch, alder, ash, bird-cherry and wych-elm trees cluster about the two streams, the Honddu and the Nant-y-Bwch, and the slopes, sheep runs or grazing for Welsh hill-ponies, are "covered with coarse grass, heather or ling, bracken and bilberry" (CGL 89). These slopes rise steeply and barely up from the depths of the valley and the impression is of forbidding starkness. The lane that takes you climbing up beyond the monastery brings you to the upper slopes of high, uninhabited moorland the remoteness of which can seem either serene and restful, or awesome, unrelenting and frightening. Around Capel-y-ffin there is both a feeling of freedom and, paradoxically, of claustrophobia.

The monastery itself is built on the side of the valley that gets less sun, accounting for Petra Tegetmeier's memory of it as "gloomy"(CON). Gill himself, in his *Autobiography*, speaks of mountains not only "above and around" Capel but, significantly, "confronting the monastery" (218); Capel was clearly viewed as a challenge and a stand. It represented a kind of freedom and it presented all kinds of almost welcome complications.

So what led Gill to such a beautiful yet testing place as the 'Chapel-at-the- end' or the 'Chapel-on-the-boundary' where, as Gerald du Barri noted, "It rains a lot.....because of the mountains, the winds blow strong and in winter it is always capped with clouds"? (JW 97)

Eric Gill, an energetic and restless soul, cast about in the early years of his maturity for a regimen that would validate and accommodate his particular blend of bohemianism. Born in 1882, Gill was the second of thirteen children, part of a family large enough, in fact, to form a small community itself! Their houses were tiny and Gill's subsequently incestuous relationships with two of his sisters were perhaps excited by the claustrophobic confines of childhood. Gill's father was a minister and his grandfather, great uncle and three of his siblings were missionaries, so there was evidently a proselytizing strain in the family. As a student and young letter-cutter Gill began to associate his developing ideas about art and workmanship with larger theories of society. In his early years in London he flirted with Fabianism and came increasingly under the influence of ideas that were shared by members of what Gill considered to be the less than satisfactory Arts and Crafts Movement, ideas which derived ultimately from Ruskin, Morris and Carlyle. Morris's dictum that true manufacture (*manu factum* = made by hand) derived from "direct communication between a man's hand and his brain" (MW XXIII 94) underpinned the 'little revolution" that Gill felt he was starting. He "was re-uniting what should never have been separated: the artist as man of imagination and the artist as workman".(AUT 162)

To enable his family to escape from the iniquities of London (to which, as we shall see, he was nonetheless willing to expose himself) Gill moved to Ditchling in 1907 and at length founded a Guild in 1921 with Hilary Pepler, who had set up a printing press in the village, and with Desmond Chute, an ex art student who was destined for the church. As Gill described it, this was a "company of craftsmen" who were "united not merely by a common desire to further the interests of their work but by the common acceptance of a rule or way of life" (AUT 206). This way of life was to be a Christian one as,before the guild began,both Gill and Pepler had become Catholics. Gill considered that this form of belief offered the opportunity of philosophically reconciling flesh and spirit. Catholicism is, after all, sensual; at the heart of its belief and practice lies the almost fetishistic consumption of bread transubstantiated into body. Communion is carnal, and Gill wrote, "just as physical love is the centre of our life as men and women, so the Holy Mass is the centre of our life as Christians" (AUT 246). Perhaps it is not insignificant that during the time Gill was being instructed in Catholicism he was carving a marble copy of his penis (MAC 115).

The patriarchal determination of Christianity suited Gill who needed women to cushion him, to do for him and to satisfy his prerogatorial phallic demands. In this light, Gill's habit of appending large or prominent genitals to his crucifixes appears as more than a mischievous schoolboy prank; it suggests a wish to assert phallocraticism. Under such a dispensation, women could actually be enslaved or exploited while the image of the Virgin Mary who transcended what was held to be the dark, destabilizing carnality of women, was ever Virgin and offered a salving focus for sentimental attachment and veneration. Mary, the desexualized woman, is venerated to mask the phallocentric prerogatives of an essentially male order. Interestingly, Gill's wife took the name of Mary when she became a Catholic at the same time as her husband, and although she appears to have been far from ever-Virgin (rather "Always ready and willing" AUT 132) she was the focus of an attachment that sentimentally esteemed her while at the same time Gill carried on duplicitous sexual relations at very close quarters. And Mary Gill appears to have been understanding, blessedly patient and ever forgiving in respect of Gill's sexual distress and self-indulgence.

The relative isolation of Ditchling's rural location provided the first in a sequence of domains (Ditchling, Capel and Pigotts) in which Gill's almost insatiable sexual curiosity could run riot. This led him into acts considered to be criminal such as incest with minors (at Ditchling) and bestiality (at Pigotts) (MAC 155-6, 239). Sexual curiosity was a continual source of excitement and pleasure but the more extreme experimentation gave rise to self-torment and bewilderment as Gill somewhat absurdly sought to justify his sexual excesses by Catholicism's reconciliation of the body and the spirit. That both these entities were good was one of the claims that Gill wanted to make in an abandoned erotic novel which he started writing in a notebook which he purchased while at Capel:

> A man soul and body — the former the form of the latter... Mind and body — both real and both good — the two naturally inseparable. (WAC)

This novel's insistence on the goodness of the material involved lengthy celebrations of urination and even one of defaecation:

> Turning he looked down at the dung he had left — already flies were buzzing and settling on it — Bright, glistening irridescent wings.(WAC)

Matter held to be gross was being celebrated; all material creation was good.

When the Ditchling community began to grow and become increasingly public, Capel-y-ffin presented the opportunity of getting even further away from civilization and from too much scrutiny; it promised a smaller unit over which Gill could preside unchallenged.

In his early life, David Jones had experienced none of Gill's political restlessness. Born in 1895, his father a printer's manager and his mother an accomplished amateur artist, Jones was attracted at a very early age by drawing and painting. Backward at reading and writing, he started his formal artistic training at fourteen and a half and his preoccupations were largely those of the aspiring artist. One subject that Jones particularly enjoyed drawing as a child was "imaginary Welshmen on hillsides with wolf-hounds" (DJL) and from as early as six years old Jones realized that he "belonged" to his father's people (DYG 23).

As he matured, Jones had a growing awareness that this heritage had been denied to him both historically and familially as his father had been deliberately anglicized by his grandfather, John Jones, a master-plasterer who lived in that town with an oddly isolated Catholic shrine, Holywell in Clwyd. James Jones, the painter's father, and David Jones himself belonged to those generations when the speaking of Welsh was looked upon as a disadvantage in a world increasingly coming under the domination of the international economic agencies of monopoly capitalism. During the First World War Jones served on the western front in the London Welsh Battalion of the Royal Welsh Fusiliers and the polarization of the complement of this battalion sharpened Jones's awareness of the respective qualities of the English and the Welsh. As he wrote in the Preface to *In Parenthesis*, that masterpiece about the trenches:

> These came from London. Those from Wales. Together they bore
> in their bodies the genuine tradition of the Island of Britain, from
> Bendigeid Vran to Jingle and Marie Lloyd. (IP x)

After the war Jones went to Westminster School of Art to continue his training. While still a student he was taken to Ditchling and introduced to Gill, returning some months later to live and work there. By 1924 he had become engaged to Gill's second daughter, Petra, enjoying a remarkable and quite untypical approval from the proprietorial Gill himself.

Throughout his life Jones was absorbed by the actual processes and *raison d'être* of so-called 'fine art', by the seeming paradox of the gratuitous necessity of art and its relation to the spiritual or emotional needs of people (Gill, by contrast, was more concerned with the usefulness of art in relation to life). Jones's knowledge of Catholicism and his comprehension of post-impressionist theory had developed almost simultaneously. When the post-impressionists asserted that the spectator should be made aware of the paint on the canvas and that the paint should transubstantiate the subject into another mode of being (i.e. the subject under the form of paint), Jones discerned a similarity with the Mass which represents the Body of Christ impanated, the Body itself being present but, as with a painting, in another mode of being. Jones was not so much preoccupied with what is popularly understood by 'art for art's sake', against which Gill was virulent in his attacks, but with art as a sign or a series of signs that guide the mind, enlarge the perception or understanding and permit the possibility of joy and also, of course, of sorrow. Jacques Maritain, the neo-Thomist French philosopher who had an important influence on Gill and Jones, wrote that signs invest social life with a meaning, giving it "an intellectual and indeed a poetical quality" (RT 220-1). And if the artist searched out signs that were valid for a particular society he searched for such signs in the orbit of his own experience or psyche. The process was one of mediation between the self and the surrounding world. It became as much a search for the artist to locate his self in the bewildering circumstances of the present as it was a search for external, universally life-enhancing signs. Gill tended to diminish this interplay. He thought that the artist should be a self-effacing workman who in the industrialized capitalist world of the twentieth century worked against the mechanical forces of plutocratic civilization. Gill's crusade was against art as a specialized activity and against the artist as "the flower of a dying civilization, the over-ripe fruit of its rotting tree" (AUT 47). Part of the idea behind an establishment such as Capel-y-ffin was that "Art must be abolished" (ESS 57). Perhaps, to judge from his oeuvre, Gill succeeded in this aim in a manner that he did not quite intend. The major qualitative difference between Gill and Jones is that Gill, the workman, was driven to produce a vast and consequently often unsubtle output whereas Jones was prepared to take the time to wrestle with problems of content and aesthetic form.

At Ditchling Gill had provided Jones with a home and a place to work as well as a fertile environment for the development of his thinking about the processes of art, so it is not surprising that shortly after Gill moved to Capel Jones should follow.

3. 1924:
'Mere geographical circumstance'

Amid the deteriorating situation at Ditchling, Gill recorded in his diary on 22 April 1924 that he went for a walk with David Jones and talked about the young man's 'engagement' to his eighteen-years-old daughter Petra, noting that, as he and his wife agreed to the arrangement, the young couple were "very happy". Two days later there was a formal betrothal in the chapel after Compline and Fr. John O'Connor wrote out a document which was signed in the sacristy after the ceremony. Cecil Gill later surmised that "Petra, in her quiet and sweet acceptance of everything and everybody accepted David Jones". He didn't "imagine that she was frantically in love with him" although he believed that Jones "was very devoted to her" (CG/DK WAC). On the day after the ceremony Gill records that Jones was received into the Craft Guild of St. Joseph and St. Dominic but, in fact, Jones only became a postulant, a stage beyond which he never passed. When Gill later wrote to Desmond Chute to explain his secession from the Guild and added that David Jones was "also resigning" Jones noted accordingly beneath this statement in his copy of *The Letters of Eric Gill* that "there seems some mistake here for I was never a member of the Guild" (LET 131 NLW).

The rift at Ditchling had been growing for some time, culminating in Gill's decision, recorded in his diary on 29 June, "that E.G. must sever his connection" with the Guild because of Hilary Pepler's "financial methods" and because of their differing "notions of an organized community". The financial disagreements were clearly symptomatic of more fundamental questions about character, social standing and power. In notes that Gill prepared for a meeting at the Dominican Priory, Haverstock Hill on 22 July, he denounced, somewhat vitriolically, Hilary Pepler's fin-

ancial disorganization, "his brutal methods/ his dictatorial man-
ner/ his minding other people's business", and his habit of bor-
rowing indiscriminately. Gill ironically asked if it was not
possible to start a Christian way of life without £5000 (WAC).
He maintained that he had been driven to such an outspoken
attack by Pepler's reaction to his decision to buy a private house
near Llanthony, for it was during this period of dispute and re-
crimination that Gill had begun to see the Ewyas valley as a
personal alternative to the Ditchling set-up. Originally it had
been considered as a possible relocation for the Guild and Pepler
had even devised a complicated scheme by which his parents
would buy a farm ostensibly for his own son David but which
would actually be for the use of the whole community. Somewhat
wary of Pepler's complicated and apparently duplicitous "man-
agement of affairs", Gill increasingly began to conceive of the
Black Mountains as the ideal location for an independent establishment for himself and his family. As recently as mid-April
there had been correspondence between Gill and Pepler and the
Prior of Caldey about the proposed quality of community life at
Capel, but by mid-June Gill was suggesting that he rent the
house adjacent to the monastery and thirty acres of the land surrounding it independently of the Ditchling Guild.

In early July Gill was at Capel-y-ffin, finalizing domestic arrangements with Donald Attwater, an authority on Eastern rites
who, in that summer of 1924, was living with his wife in the west
wing of the monastery at Capel which housed all the amenities.
Although Gill had first heard of the Ewyas valley from Peter
Anson while on a visit to Quarr Abbey (RR 164) it was Attwater,
a chance visitor to Ditchling, who had quickened his enthusiasm.
There was a juggling of possibilities about where everyone
should fit in, and as Gill wished to move in August he was keen
to receive a swift acceptance of his proposal that the monastery
be let to him for £50 till Christmas, when a more formal undertaking would come into effect.

Back at Ditchling on 11 July, Gill began the lengthy process of
sorting books. He formally resigned from the Guild on 22 July
and the end of the month and the beginning of August were taken
up with packing; his workshop alone took five days to sort.

The previous months had clearly been taxing and during this
period Gill resorted to one of his most extreme forms of comfort

which, at the same time, was itself cause for distress. From the evidence of deleted diary entries, Gill was indulging in anal intercourse and mutual masturbation with his eldest daughter, Elizabeth (D 19.3 & 22.5.24). This could no longer be rationalized as 'experiment' as it had been four years previously — though even then Gill recorded that such behaviour "must stop"(D 12.1.20); this was the disturbing and potentially harmful indulgence of a man under stress. Significantly, in a letter to his daughters in Rome on Papal pilgrimage in the following year, Gill wrote: "Implore a blessing for us also. Tell him I am very sorry for my sins. You, especially, Elizabeth, are to tell him that" (15.7.25 WAC).

As Gill attempted to tidy up or skate over the obvious licence of such incidents so he later brushed over the whole unpleasant episode of his break with Ditchling in which, it seems, his behaviour had been less than exemplary:

> "Perhaps I left the brethren rather in the lurch but that was no fault of mine because the scheme had been for the whole lot of us to leave Ditchling and re-establish ourselves in Wales..."(AUT 216).

Certainly Pepler's affadavit, sworn in August 1926 against Gill's subsequent legal action, maintained that Gill "deserted the scheme" and "left liabilities on the shoulders of myself and others associated with us". Whereas Gill specified that Pepler was indebted to him for the sum of £182 4s 5d, Pepler claimed that Gill was indebted to him "in a much larger sum in connection with the said scheme than the amount which he claims in this Action" (WAC).

Despite the acrimony, the seemingly insuperable and mounting suspicion and resentment, there was a nominal reconciliation which took the form of a picnic on the downs after which the Gills departed on 13 August.

The move to Capel was not cheap. Excluding travel the cost came to £101, an enormous sum in 1924. Three families made the trip: the Gills who left behind their middle daughter Petra to learn weaving, the Brennans who were farm workers and the engraver Philip Hagreen and his wife Aileen. These were given a "fine welcome" and found not only the Attwaters in the west wing of the monastery but also Fr. Joseph Woodford, a monk from

Caldey who was convalescing in the mountains along with Brother Raphael Davies who cared for him. With these monks was a "tall, handsome, pale young man, with spectacles and wild black hair" (FA 100) who had been at Ampleforth and had recently decided against a Jesuit novitiate. This was René Hague, destined to become Gill's son-in-law and one of Jones's closest friends. In August 1924 Hague was instructing Brother Davies in the classics and was eagerly awaiting the arrival of the Gills as he had heard about their unattached daughter Joanna, who was, in fact, only fourteen years old at the time:

> "This great caravan came up the road, I remember very well because I was...cutting sticks up on the hill...and I came dashing down, and people poured out of the lorry — goats and hens and rabbits and— girls..."(BBCHRC)

Hague and the two monks lived in the Grange, a house that Fr. Ignatius had originally built for his mother and which stood a little apart from the monastery. This would also now provide an immediate home for the Brennans. The Attwaters remained in the west wing of the monastery itself, the Gills settled in most of the east and south wings and the Hagreens occupied what was left.

The monastery had been built in local sandstone, painted white and roofed with slate and tile. In his book on Eric Gill, *A Cell of Good Living*, Donald Attwater gives a good account of the interior. On the ground floor the rooms were of "various shapes and sizes, mostly opening into one another, and with fireplaces which had to be very drastically dealt with" (CGL 92). These never proved satisfactory for they had been modified to burn coal whereas the Gills habitually burnt wood. The upshot was that the atmosphere could be very smoky and this, combined with sewers that easily blocked, could readily give the impression, as it did to Peter Anson, that Capel was even less comfortable than Ditchling. The ground floor of the monastery had high ceilings with exposed beams, creating a great sense of space, while the upper floors of the east and north wings, apart from several normal bedrooms, comprised two long rows of monastic 'cells' made of pitch pine:

> "These cubicles — or loose-boxes — were uniform, each just large

enough to accommodate a narrow bed, a chair and a small table, and each lit by a tiny window. The wooden partitions of these apartments were only seven feet high, with a liberal space of open roof above them." (CGL 92)

The internal structuring of these upper floors could therefore easily be adapted.

Work began almost immediately to turn the north cloisters into a temporary chapel. And Donald Attwater, who along with all his other talents was "an excellent glazier", set about repairing all the lead windows in the monastery 'of which there were dozens" (AUT 228). From the evidence of a letter written to Desmond Chute a month after arriving at Capel, it seems that Gill had ambitious plans to re-roof Fr. Ignatius's church that stood beside the monastery and which had fallen into grave disrepair, but these plans were never realized (LET 181/2).

A pattern of Mass and Communion at 6.30 to 7.00 a.m. was quickly established and otherwise the early days at Capel were taken up with work about the monastery and with exploratory walks. A milk float was purchased at the end of August for £10 and it was to prove a useful and acceptably unmechanical form of transport. By contrast, Brother Davies had a 1913 Austro-Daimler, a vehicle that didn't quite square with Gill's vision of what was necessary to life in a secluded mountain setting.

In a letter of mid-September to Desmond Chute, Gill noted that "Everyone in this valley is most kind and friendly" and that his children "are of course much occupied with the work of this new life" (LET 182). Elizabeth the eldest daughter, was particularly well equipped to deal with the challenge of Capel as she had worked in a small family hotel in Gruyères several years before. Gill's wife, Mary, with her penchant for amateur farming, was likewise well disposed to face the situation.

If the neighbours had proved friendly the weather, on the other hand, had been less than welcoming; Philip Hagreen wrote to Chute in mid-September:

"I hope that we are not having normal weather. Since we came there have been two days without rain. Most days it has rained heavily. A strong and icy wind has blown almost continually. We have had sunshine of great beauty, but devoid of warmth" (GLE 16.9.24).

28

1. The Ewyas Valley

2. The Monastery, Capel-y-ffin

An early visitor who was to spend much time at Capel and considerably embellish its life was Dom Theodore Bailey from Caldey Island. Dom Theodore had studied painting in Paris under the post-impressionist Maurice Denis. It was Denis who had lucidly expressed the idea that underpins the work of the post-impressionists when he stated that "a picture is essentially a flat surface covered with an arrangement of colour". While Denis's aesthetics had some points of affinity with Gill's notions about art, perhaps his capacity, evident in some of his paintings, for an oversweetened religiosity did not prove to be the best example for Dom Theodore to follow. Gill liked Bailey very much and discerned a rapid improvement in his woodcuts during Bailey's first stay at Capel. On the other hand, David Jones did not have much admiration for Dom Theodore's work, yet he, like everybody else who lived at or visited Capel-y-ffin, profited from Bailey's thorough knowledge of Thomism which formed the basis of Gill's thinking about art.

What with unpacking, sorting, exploring and the arrival of various visitors, Gill did not get down to his own work for about a month. To Desmond Chute on 11 September Gill wrote that

> "Until this week I have hardly done a stroke of work except the work of house arranging & fitting etc. Now, at last I am able to start again & must keep at it henceforth like anything. I've got plenty to do I am glad to say." (LET 180).

Indeed from the day after that letter was written until 1 October Gill was carving *Deposition* in a cellar workshop which provided a dim and damp substitute for a previous, temporary studio which had been separated from the Attwater's living room only by a curtain (SPE 154). *Deposition* was taken to London on 6 October and sold by the Goupil Gallery for £90. Gill spent eight days in London staying with David Jones's family in Brockley which he enjoyed "very much" for he considered Jones's father and mother to be "most kind and hospitable" (LET 150). It is interesting to speculate on the impact that the smocked and eccentric Gill made on the essentially nineteenth century lower-middle-class domestic pride and order of the home of Jones's parents in Howson Road, Brockley. How would Mr Jones, involved with typographical mass-production on the *Christian*

Herald, have reacted to the opinions of the apparently quasi-Luddite Gill?

One evening during his stay, Gill records that he talked with David Jones about "art & work" (D 12.10.24). The subject matter would seem to have been so habitual between the two men that it is surprising that it is even recorded, for what else would they talk about other than "art and work"? Perhaps the discussion related to the fact that three days earlier Gill had talked with William Marchant of the Goupil Gallery "re D.J." (D 9.10.24). Gill already had a high opinion of the gifts of the younger man and now that Jones was to be a son-in-law perhaps an active helping hand was being offered.

Gill's time in London was obviously not confined to Brockley; the pattern of these frequent trips to the capital was crushed and crowded. This time Gill visited the Tate with David Jones who always found it a "somewhat unsympathetic gallery" though he was "not able to decide why" (LSL NLW). Gill spent a day with Jones and his daughter Petra who visited from Ditchling and he walked on Hampstead Heath with Fr. Vincent McNabb. On 14 October Jones accompanied Gill to Paddington to see him off back to Capel-y-ffin.

Homecomings were marked by the necessity of answering letters and on this occasion that activity was followed by a period of miscellaneous engraving and the preparation of prints for the Society of Wood Engravers Exhibition. Gill produced, among other things, a sensitive zinc engraving of Gordian, his seven year old adopted son, who had taken his first communion at Capel in mid-September. Gill also discussed the subject of "industrialism" and "labour politics" with Fr. Joseph Woodford as he was engaged on an engraved 'cartoon' called *Safety First* for the *Labour Woman* which was subsequently reprinted in *The Daily Herald*.

In mid-November Mary Gill went to Chichester to visit her mother and to Brighton to attend the auction of Hopkins Crank which had been the Gill's abode at Ditchling. The house was sold for £1850 and as Gill put it in one of his many letters to Desmond Chute devoted to the Ditchling wrangle, "As we spent, of our own money, on the place something over £1500 and there was a mortgage of £900, you will see that it was not exactly a profitable deal" (24.5.25 GLE).

Despite spending November evenings with René Hague reading and discussing Maritain's *The Philosophy of Art*, evenings that "coloured" Hague's "whole life" (BBC HRC), and despite "the daily companionship and fellow conspiratorship of Donald Attwater" (AUT 221), Gill wrote to Desmond Chute as early on as his third month at Capel to say that "I'm a bit lonely — sometimes v. much so" (LET 183). The inclement weather was having an adverse effect upon Philip Hagreen's fragile health and he was "too ill to discuss much" (LET 183). What is more, there was an unfortunate clash of character between Gill and Hagreen's intellectual wife. Gill, who at the best of times found "it very difficult to see the other person's point of view" (BBC HRC RH) did not consider discussion with women to be possible. In any case, it seems that the women were too busy at Capel running their domestic support system to have had much opportunity for discussion. The patriarchal pattern is one that Gill had learnt in his childhood home; while his mother "worried and fought and sweated, while she worked her fingers to the bone with sewing and washing and mending and cleaning" (AUT 45) his father went on with his writing and reading. Significantly in 'An Epitaph', one of the poems that Gill's sister Enid Clay had written for her collection, *Sonnets & Verses*, a dying woman proclaims that

> "I am going
> To where there's no washing or cooking or sewing".

It is not so much that the women's tasks at Capel were considered to be on a lower plane than those of the men, it is just that certain time-consuming duties were unquestionably designated to that sex and it prohibited them from participating fully in the cerebral or more self-consciously creative activities with which the men occupied themselves.

From 24 to 29 November Gill was again in London, this time accompanied by René Hague and joined for a short while by his wife. Gill's first visit was to the St George's Gallery to deliver prints for the Society of Wood Engravers Exhibition and there he met Noel Rooke and Paul Nash. Again Gill saw a lot of David Jones; on the evening of 26 November they attended a lecture on ancient crucifixes and on the following day they went to look at copper plate presses. Mary Gill returned to Capel before her husband and on the night of 28 November John Rothenstein took notes from Gill for his introduction to a forthcoming book on the artist's work. This session went on into the small hours and Gill, obviously animated by their talk, remained awake till 5 a.m. reading Lawrence's *Sons and Lovers*. The next day he drew a portrait of Rachel Rothenstein and had sufficient energy left to go to spend an "exhilarating" weekend with Robert Gibbings (who ran the Golden Cockerel Press) and his wife Moira at Waltham St Lawrence near Twyford in Berkshire. Gill "drew Mrs Gibbings (nude)" (D. 30.11.24) while he and Robert Gibbings, a six foot three inch tall reddish blonde Irishman, also sat in the nude. Again the next morning he was drawing Moira Gibbings in the nude yet, by contrast, on the following day, in an act of filial piety, Gill drew his mother's portrait for a birthday present. Whereas his nudes tend to be cold or anonymous bodies this drawing was an affectionate and loving study of a cognizable person.

Back at Capel for five days Gill was largely occupied with letter writing before leaving, with Mary, for a two-day visit to Caldey Island. After a very wet crossing, Gill made some drawings of the roof of Caldey Parish church for the community for which he made no charge, drew a portrait of Fr. Prior and discussed, with Dom Columba, the subject of Catholicism and capitalism; Gill's writings reveal that he was wary of the dangerous affiliations between a clergy that was all too eager to be materially comfortable and a consumer society that actually lived in contradiction to its professed Christian principles.

Already, despite the long uninterrupted early periods spent at Capel (from 14 August to 6 October and 14 October to 24 November), a pattern of getting away, either for work of for pleasure, begins to emerge. The increasingly frequent sorties over the ensuing months somewhat challenge the assertion that Mary Gill made in a letter to Desmond Chute: "It is beautiful here in the Welsh mountains...we love the Monastery — and it is extraordinary how little the outside world seems to matter" (SPE 155).

Back at Capel on 9 December, Gill fixed up his new copper plate press and printed the children's portraits and Christmas cards. By the time it drew towards Christmas the inhabitants had settled into the pattern of their new life. Donald Attwater records that the evening meal was taken by candlelight on a long narrow scrubbed table and that while food was being served Gill would read from the Martyrology which "tended to promote hilarity, even ribaldry, rather than the intended edification" (CGL 109). Afterwards, a guest or one of the daughters would read from the epistle and this would often provoke interesting conversation. Attwater suggests that these proceedings were "quite unaffected" (CGL 109) although Speaight contradictorily suggests that the impression made by Gill's household could be one of "affectation". The excellent point that Gill himself makes about their style of life at Capel-y-ffin is that

> "we were compelled by mere geographical circumstance to live in a way which would have been fantastically heroic and unnatural and pedantic in any place less remote from industrial civilization." (AUT 228).

The awkward location of Capel provided Gill's favoured style of life with a *raison d'être*.

On 22 December David Jones and Norval Gray, the nephew of the symbolist poet and priest Fr. John Gray, arrived. Petra Gill came from Ditchling on the same day and was met by her sister Joanna at Abergavenny where they both stayed for the night. By 24 December family and friends were assembled for their first Capel Christmas. Petra Tegetmeier recalls that at the festival they went around the valley carol singing (CON) and certainly song was important at Capel; René Hague recalled that he heard a multitude of folk songs while he was living there and some of these found their way into the fabric of Jones's later poetry. Gill himself maintained that his daughters knew "simply hundreds of songs and sang them in trio" (AUT 235). This particular Christmas Eve there was a two and a quarter hour choir practice prior to the carol singing in the valley which was followed by a "Glorious Midnight Mass (Singing and Incense!)" (D 24.12.24). On Christmas Day there was a second Mass at 9 a.m., then a third with carols and Compline and carols at 6 p.m. After dinner there was time for games and presents.

During the following days there were more games and the Gills took walks with David Jones and Petra. Eric Gill also talked with René Hague about his future and read Maritain with David Jones and Donald Attwater. 1924 ended quietly — except that the singing went on into the new year!

4. Philosophy
and Pamphleteering

Essential to our understanding of the lifestyle and the work done at Capel-y-ffin is some acquaintance with certain tenets of neo-Thomist aesthetic thinking, and I shall relate my comments on this subject to the ideas expressed by Gill in the pamphlets that he wrote during this period. That there appears something medieval about the set-up at Capel-y-ffin is due not only to the fact that Gill sought an alternative to the post-industrial degradations of life but also to the fact that the source of Gill's aesthetic position is to be found in Jacques Maritain's mediation of Thomist ideas. Aquinas, with his "somewhat mathematical, precise... 'black and white'...method of setting out and drawing conclusions" was, as Cecil Gill suggested, the "kind of teaching authority" which suited his brother Eric's way of thinking (CG/DK WAC). Jacques Maritain's aesthetics which derived from St. Thomas were the basis for debate at Capel-y-ffin as they had been at Ditchling, after the printing there of Fr John O'Connor's translation of *Arte et Scholastique* into *The Philosophy of Art* in 1923. This work, in its attempt to give pertinence to Thomist principles, worked in accordance with the broad ambition of Neo-Thomism which was at the height of its influence among English Catholics during the 1920s.

Attwater suggests that for Gill *The Philosophy of Art* "became an armoury of weapons" (CGL 114) but David Jones later warned of the dangers of a too rigid application of the ideas or rules that he had learnt from Maritain and Gill:

> "Such definitions could only have indeed a damaging effect on the making of things if thought of as providing some sort of theory to work by — a substitute for imagination" (DJL)

and such misuse of these principles is something to which Eric Gill was evidently disposed.

Gill's thinking about art and society had also been influenced by the Anglo-Ceylonese aesthetician Ananda Coomaraswamy, who had personal experience of a society that lived by the skill of its hands and also, as a result of western imperialism, experience of the swift destruction of that society. Coomaraswamy was well placed to observe the west's "exaggerated standards of living, and equally depreciated standards of life" (COPA 62). Gill was further influenced by John Ruskin and William Morris who looked back beyond the recent industrialized system to a medieval dispensation where making was contrived by a skilled artisan using "direct communication between...hand and...brain" (MW XXIII 94). Behind Ruskin and Morris stood Thomas Carlyle and the whole Romantic reaction to industrialization and the Romantic development of the concept of alienation by such writers as Herder, Schiller and Novalis.

Before we consider Gill's discussion of aesthetics between 1924 and 1928 it would be appropriate to note why Gill fashioned a particular lifestyle at Capel-y-ffin and to observe how it squared with his vision of an ideal life. Whatever we may think of Gill's work or his moral inconsistencies, his thinking about industrialism and its deformations and consequences is clear, direct, just and of great and increasing importance. Gill observed that industrialism, which denies to workmen the capacity to make choices and reduces them to a state of unthinking irresponsibility, gives rise to universal slavery. Gill had no dislike of machines *per se*, in fact he was often attracted by their functional beauty, but he detested the way in which they enslaved people and made ever increasing profitability the prime concern of capitalist existence. Instead of a situation in which artisans controlled their tools by means of their artistry Gill found a society in which machines enslaved people in order to make profit for a few. Gill envisaged a time approaching when

> "the arts of agriculture and the farm, the arts of the kitchen, clothes, furniture, pottery and metal, the whole business of building — from cottages to cathedrals — all these things will be made or done by machines, and we shall be released for 'higher things'. So they say. But for the majority of men and women — for us — there are *no higher things*". (WP 139-40)

It is the practice of art, taken in its widest sense (the intellectual habit that guides what is to be made), which distinguishes mankind from the other species. Gill reacted against the narrow definition of art which conceived of culture as something "added like a sauce"; by contrast he noted that throughout history, a true and vital culture "has been the product of the work men did for their livings" (BLAH 203). In the twentieth century, after over one hundred years of industrialism, commercialism and the consequent abnormal growth of cities, society at large was engaged upon the relentless struggle for unlimited quantities of material goods while the degraded nature of its existence allowed no time or the development of its latent intellectual or creative powers.

Gill considered that the end of industrialism was inevitable, for in the "leisure state" to which industrialism had given rise people don't really "*love* the 'good things' they...enjoy in such plenty...in reality they...despise everything". Things are "made for passing enjoyment, to be scrapped when no longer enjoyable" (LE 71). We can see Gill's vision confirmed as we look at the capitalist empires and megalopoli of the second half of the century; capacity for love has clearly been undermined by such a system when even people are considered to be "for passing enjoyment, to be scrapped when no longer enjoyable".

The labour unrest that Gill observed in, say, the General Strike of 1926 he attributed not, as the contemptuous and avaricious employers did, "to the unbridled greed of workmen" but to the workers's "instinctive, if inarticulate, desire for freedom and responsibility" (ISL 21). One of the first ways in which the industrial situation could be changed would be for the ownership of the means of production to pass from the banks and the large corporations to the workers themselves. The right of ownership "does not derive from man's need to use things but from his need to *make* things. As a moral being, purely as such, man has no right of private ownership" (LET 358). Gill advocated, therefore, not possession for its own sake but as a kind of tenancy. People were merely denied control of their work because they served the profit-making drives of some distant capitalist who was not interested in making good things but in making money. If people owned their own means of production then they would be responsible for their own work. In a letter to *G.K.'s Weekly* of 27

August 1927, Gill allies himself with the Distributists who "are fighting for the rights of working men — their right of property and of ownership in their work — against the tyranny of men of commerce" (GKW 578). Gill proposed that the ideal life should be one of holy poverty — not the poverty of deprivation but a state that induced a rational attitude towards the material world, and that notion embraces everything from the idea that man extends the work of creation by the habit of making to a responsible ecological awareness and care. Life at Capel at least afforded the opportunity for its inhabitants and visitors to pursue their work in a condition of holy poverty. It also offered a suitable environment for the philosophical contemplation of the activity that preoccupied all the residents (including the farmers and the cooks), the habit of art.

Never one to become needlessly bogged down in metaphysics, what Gill sought in Thomism was a set of rules, an approach that would give him a method by which to proceed. Gill was above all a workman, he worked to time like an artisan, costing by the hour and, humbly, at a very reasonable rate. When the aesthetic discussions became intensely metaphysical we can suppose that strong contributions were made by Dom Theodore Bailey who comprehended the "whole system of the Schoolmen" (RH DJ 27), by the boisterous energy of René Hague's intellect, and by David Jones's meandering curiosity. At any rate, in the Prologue to Gill's first polemical essay to be published while he was at Capel, *Id Quod Visum Placet*, these people are acknowledged for their "help and criticism" for the essay was the direct result of debates between them.

The problem posed by the essay ('that which being seen pleases') is obviously to define the quality of the pleasure to which the title refers. Beautiful things by definition please and therefore what is beauty? In *Art Nonsense and Other Essays* published in the year after he left Capel, Gill wrote that "Beauty is an Essential Perfection of Creation and of handiwork" (AN 3); in both instances it is the marriage of the good and true. "Beauty", writes Maritain, is "an object of the intelligence, for that which *knows* in the full sense of the word is the intelligence, which alone is open to the infinity of Being" (PA 33).

Now for the intellect to recognize or comprehend the revelation of beauty, St. Thomas laid down three conditions: integrity, proportion and clarity. This last condition is also called by St. Thomas, "*splendor formae*" which Maritain explains as "the principle which makes the proper perfection of all that is, which upbuilds and completes things in their essence and in their qualities, which is, in a word, if one may so say, Being, purely such..." (PA 35). Beauty is both the revelation of essence and the actual determination of the thing itself. It results from the successful liaison between the mind of the maker, the material and the circumstances or demands of the work in hand. Beauty resides in aptness which has been determined by formal choice.

Gill lucidly distinguishes form from mere shape: "Shape is only the visible aspect of form. The soul of a thing is its form" (AUT 83). So we may be attracted by mere shape, something that may be lovely and that may satisfy a physical desire, but the activity of art is concerned with matters more complex than the merely lovely. Beauty, writes Maritain, "is the lofty delectation of the mind, which is quite the contrary of what is called pleasure, or the pleasant tickling of the sensitive side" (PA 95). What is visible in Gill's own work is a confusion between the ambition to reveal beauty (which he achieves in his lettering) and his tendency to become absorbed in "pleasant tickling" (the published nudes).

The idea of the revelation of essence by *splendor formae* suggested that a work of art was not a representation of a thing but the essence of the thing itself in another mode of being: "the painting is the subject — the subject made in paint rather than represented in paint" (IQ 13-14); the proximity to Maurice Denis's post-impressionist dictum is obvious.

In *Id Quod* Gill stresses that the artist must not be concerned with the effect of his work upon the viewer but only with the demands placed upon the maker himself by the thing which he wishes to make. It is the job of the artist to order his inspiration in such a way as to reveal form or essence. Maritain writes that integrity or proportion "have no absolute significance, and must be understood solely in relation to the aim of the work, which is to induce the splendor of form upon the matter" (PA 40-1). Now it must be noted that this revelation, unlike the purely formal questions of integrity and proportion, inevitably possesses moral implications.

The artist's ability to reveal form is developed by the intellectual habit of the practice of art. This Maritain suggests is easily pursued under the master/apprentice mode of the middle ages, a procedure readily espoused at Ditchling and Capel-y-ffin:

> "the natural gift is only a condition prerequisite to art, or a natural inchoation of the artistic *habitus*. This spontaneous disposition is evidently indispensable; but without a culture and a discipline which the ancients required to be long and patient and honest, it will never grow into art properly so called" (PA 61).

Once the artist has served his "apprentice education, the working novitiate under a master" (PA 62) he becomes a "master who uses rules according to his aims" (PA 57), or, in other words, according to his judgement since art is *"the right deduction from things to be made"(recta ratio factibilium)* (PA 10). The habit of art is of paramount importance; as David Jones put it so clearly: for the artist "there is no surrogate for being 'on the job' " (E&A 12). Certainly, the development and practice of this artistic *habitus* could be said to be the *raison d'être* behind Gill's establishments at Ditchling, Capel-y-ffin and later at Pigotts.

From the evidence of the preparatory notes for *Id Quod Visum Placet* — correspondence on the subject and the re-writings (one page graced with the typical distractions of faint drawings of fellatio and arcing ejaculation caught by the mouth of a distant woman), it is obvious that Gill took great pains over the pamphlet. It was, after all, his first major public statement; he had practised various arts, he had sought philosophical bases for these activities and pondered and debated them, and by the time he came to live at Capel he had developed something to say.

The pamphlet was accordingly well received. Maritain's secretary wrote in receipt on behalf of the French philosopher who was at that time dogged by ill-health: *"M. Maritain l'a lu avec tout l'interet qu'il mérite et avec un vif plaisir"* (WAC). Ananda Coomaraswamy wrote to Gill that "I am glad you have written it. Sound ideas on the subject are too rarely propounded" (3.12.26 WAC).

In the essay *Art and Love*, published in 1927, Gill discussed the respective realms of *ars*, or making, and *prudentia*, or acting, which he had touched upon in *Id Quod Visum Placet*:

> "We speak of doing when we imply a means to an end. We speak of making when we envisage an end" (AL 4).

The discussion of this "ordering of things to be made" (AL 4) finds an echo in a passage of *The Philosophy of Art* that appears to have influenced Gill's thinking. Art

> "settles the *artifex*, artist or craftsman, in a world apart, fenced, bounded, detached, where it puts man's strength and man's intelligence and man's time at the service of a thing which he is making. That is true of every art: slackness of living and of willing stop at the door of every workshop" (PA 8).

This means that theoretically Gill's moral sloppiness or self-indulgence could be held apart from his performance as an artist. However David Jones, in an unpublished draft, wrote about Gill's "preoccupation with 'this flesh' somewhat diagrammatically expressed" which gave "a kind of slickness to certain of his works" (NLW 1978 DEP V/16). When Jones went on to observe that this "did *not* damage his total integrity and central Christianity as a man" we can only suppose that Jones could have known but a little of the self-torment to which Gill's enormities gave rise while also noting that Jones immediately perceived the effects of the obsessions of the man on the works of the artist.

Gill wrote in *Art and Love* that "The worship that art implies is simply that by which a man devotes himself to the well-making of the thing to be made" (AL 5). But is it sufficient to invoke St. Augustine's "Love God and make what you will" (*'Dilige Deum et fac quod vis'*) if what you make in fact discloses the aberrations and obsessions of a personality which Maritain maintained should be left behind at the studio door? Perhaps what we repeatedly observe in Gill's work is that humility, which should be content to rest in a kind of unknowingness and which should be the *sine qua non* of art, is being overidden by a certain proselytizing display of sexuality or by a phallocratic need to pin God down. As the form is or reveals the soul, so the form of the work reflects and reveals ideas that emanate from the maker — in Gill's case a maker either compulsively overworking or confounded by emotional and sexual pressures. Gill's published nudes often appear to have been drawn by a deliciating voyeur or to possess an almost self-protective slickness, and his sexual emphases in Christian contexts are, at times, excessive. His need to be the master is evident in the blatantly didactic nature of much

of his work and as he entertained an idiosyncratic and self-indul-
gent vision of Christianity which raised many clerical eyebrows
he was seen by some to be "the devil quoting scripture". Fr. Austin who taught logic at Hawkesyard Priory took Gill to task over
the obvious dangers of a position which advocated 'Love God
and make what you like'. Austin stressed the practical impossibility of the philosophical distinction between art and prudence:

> "for every living artist *is* an ethical teacher — and none more emphatic
> and dogmatic than yourself.... Surely you have not so misunderstood
> your Maritain, as to suppose that there can be any *human* activity,
> any human production, that is neither good nor evil..." (WAC
> 3.11.27).

The work of art is not an end in itself for once it exists it will
affect others. So while it is not the means to an end (except
perhaps what Maritain later defined as *"the end beyond any end"*
[CIAP 170] of beauty) it will have a transitive effect. Fr. Austin
urged

> "that man is a unity — that making things is a fruit growing out of
> that unity; that man being a unity, will make things according as he
> knows and wills" (WAC 3.11.27).

That this is so is marked by the *Times Literary Supplement* review of Gill's engravings for the *Passio Domini Jesu Christi* where
the astute reviewer suggests that Gill's 'mannerisms' suggest "an
attitude rather than a style" (*TLS* 29.7.26). 'Bad art", as Gill
wrote in 'The Enormities of Religious Art', "is not unskilful — it
is skill contaminated, deprived of its proper object by folly"
(MON 1.28 42).

Gill's mother's reaction to *Id Quod Visum Placet* is illustrative
of the absurd and intransigent prudery, that legacy of Victorian
morality, which dogged English society at least until midway
through our century:

> "And.....why have you put a naked man in the frontispiece 'more to
> amuse than to elevate or instruct'? It will keep me from passing the
> book round in the circle amongst whom I live" (WAC 14.11.26).

Against such stifling prudery and "the prudent man's inclination to see in the pleasure of the sense mere filthiness" (AP 13)

was not Gill right to assert that the representation of "the physical union of lovers...in word or work is not *in itself* an evil thing" (AL 13)? However, it was his inner attitude, his own discomfort in the making public of such works that infected them with a sense of 'naughtiness' and prurience, so often rendering them less than noble. Gill's work provides adequate evidence to suggest that the end of the work is determined not only by the isolated *habitus* of art but by the state of the maker who practises that *habitus*. Man as moral being is at some level ultimately inseparable from man the maker.

Christianity and Art of 1927 throws Thomist ideas about art into a wider social context. The post-industrial enslavement of the maker is considered in relation to the destruction of artefacture whereas the possible enslavement of the maker by his own personality is not considered. *Christianity and Art* also considers the relation of the Church to art — how modern individualism and materialism have undermined people's capacity to appreciate the "spiritual", "anonymous" and "intellectual art of the Church" (CA 4). And the Church is credited with "maintaining the ideas and the attitude of mind in which alone any great art is possible" (CA 8).

Yet again in this pamphlet Gill asserts somewhat stubbornly that "beauty is independent....of ethical association" (CA 25). If a writer proclaims 'Look after goodness and truth, and beauty will take care of itself' then what would ultimately prove more profitable is not an analysis of the habit of art but rather a discussion of the qualities of 'goodness' and 'truth' which once established would provide the artist with a sound basis from which to proceed. To fall back on undefined elements such as the existence and function of the soul (*viz* CA 19), or unquestioned absolutes such as Christian belief ("hard facts") Gill had called them in *Art and Love*) is ultimately of little practical help. The *Times Literary Supplement* reviewer of *Art and Prudence* (1928) commented that Gill's "definitions are not very intricate, nor does he define every important term which he uses" (TLS 15.11.28). Perhaps Gill himself came to see his deficiencies; writing to Desmond Chute in 1928 he confessed that "I get more and more painfully aware that I ought not to be writing at all — not sufficient philosophical training" (LET 239-40). Yet Gill did not stop, going on to publish polemical writing consistently until his death in 1940 and the central irresolution between the maker, what he made and what he professed seemed to persist.

The idea that sensuousness is liberated in art by its reconciliation with reason — a central tenet of classical idealistic aesthetics (EC 184) — allows us to discern the crux of Gill's failure. His sensuality appears to have been such an overbearing and irrational force that it inhibited reconciliation with reason. Gill tried to avoid admitting this to himself and the result, in the published nudes, is fraud. Art, of course, can result when irrational pressures become so great that they distort balanced formulations. The tension between what the artist feels and what is reasonable results in a power of expression that has about it the beauty of honesty and inevitability. Gill's private erotic drawings are more real, shine with a greater *splendor formae* than those published nudes where he tries to suppress or to deny the extremity of his feelings for his subject and, as it were, gloss them over. Occasionally, in his unpublished private erotica, when Gill admits to his almost uncontrollable irrationality, he does, paradoxically, create a just and rational embodiment of what existed in his mind, untrammelled by the prettifying dishonesty of meddlesome and slickening editorial control.

Gill as a thinker and writer made some useful observations about industrialism and some challenging analyses of the process of the practice of art. But in practical fact, despite an heroic effort, he could not avoid compromise entanglements with many of the institutions that he denounced, and in his own art work there was, for the most part, an inextricable confusion between the moral idiosyncrasies of the man and the often mannered formal ambitions of the artist.

5. 1925 'A world untouched'

The beginning of 1925 seemed to characterize the best of life at Capel-y-ffin. Despite the harshness of the winter there were games, gatherings, walks, and discussions with Attwater, Hague and Jones — an exchange of philosophical ideas that marked one of the most profitable aspects of the Gillian experiment. Over the Christmas period René Hague and David Jones had become friends. Hague, who needed to rise early after he started at Chapel Farm on 12 January and who needed a pretext to take up early morning tea to Joanna Gill, was obliged to take it up to the others and remembers David Jones, the ex-soldier, receiving him in his "cell or cubicle" with "Ah, gunfire! Thank you, china" — that colourful cockney trench slang which had made such an indelible impression on the young painter during his time on the western front (DG 32). Slang and swearing of which there appears to have been a good deal at Capel would sound, to the modern ear, curiously refined; Hague and Jones gave a performance of this mannered way of speaking in front of William Blissett in 1959:

> "-Biscuit?
> -Neo, thenks very mach.
> -You mean you'll have fack-all?
> -Fack-all, thenks very mach" (LC 20).

René Hague developed the reputation of being, as David Kindersley put it, "rather over-outspoken" (CG/DK WAC) but during this period Hague noted that he "took every single thing" that Gill said "absolutely for gospel" (BBC HRC). He was working land for Gill half the time and half the time for Chapel Farm. He was not paid and could not remember having any money, but recalled that he was treated like a son and provided for (BBC

HRC).

David Jones's living conditions were more comfortable than they had been at Ditchling and he was hard at work almost as soon as he arrived. He painted a crucifixion in what had been Fr. Ignatius's Bible Cloister, was then the Chapel, and was to become Gill's workshop. He painted a metal tabernacle and did a good deal of painting, as Hague recalls, "muffled against the cold in scarf and tightly lashed trench-coat" (DG 32). Jones made engravings and box-wood carvings and he made pen and ink sketches and watercolours, one Hague notes "painted out of doors in February: a tribute to his hardiness" (DG 32). Nevertheless, Petra Tegetmeier recalls that Jones found the cold at Capel a strain and spent a lot of time ill in bed (CON).

Certainly, while Jones's output could be prolific (and this was the case at Capel and on Caldey Island) his working methods were troubled by bouts of inactivity, the result of illness, neurasthenia or artistic dissatisfaction. Whereas Gill marched swiftly, according to an efficient rule book, Jones tended to meander in a kind of fertile confusion. Moreover, Gill's notion of the necessity of having a tidy and efficient work space was uncongenial to Jones who tended to work in a degree of mess and clutter. Writing to Desmond Chute about Jones's determination to earn his living by his art (something that Jones himself, later in life, seems to have hindered by his reluctance to sell work), Gill noted that "he's so incapacitated by his temperament and unworkmanlike training" (LET 189). Of course, it should be stressed that Gill was first and foremost an artisan whereas Jones was a 'fine artist' more interested in "showing again under other forms" (E&A 155) in an art executed entirely for its own sake and with an inutile but far from useless end.

On 20 January, Gill and Jones went to meet Gill's old patron Count Kessler at Llanthony but somehow missed him. Kessler, who was born of Swiss-Irish parents, had been educated in England and lived in Germany. He was a true European, a pacifist, and years before he had tried to apprentice Gill to Aristide Maillol. When everybody eventually met at the monastery they discussed, as Gill recorded, "German politics" and his "lettering for the Vergil Book" (D 20.1.25) which involved designs by Maillol.

Kessler, for his part, recorded in his diary his impressions of "a beautiful but lonely valley between meadows and hedges" and of

Gill as being of "Tolstoyan appearance in his smock and coat, which emanated a half peasant-like, half monk-like atmosphere". In fact, the whole family would have presented a similar spectacle as they all wore garments of mixed grey, white and brown — the colour of undyed sheep's wool. Kessler recorded that Gill

> "and his wife, and also their children (which is still stranger) like it very much in the solitude of that monastery-like atmosphere. Ditchling had been too narrow-minded: they had only the choice between the wilderness and London and decided to try the wilderness first;" (SPE 165-6).

However much at that stage the family seemed contented with Capel-y-ffin, Gill himself, for professional reasons and perhaps because of certain personal inclinations was, on 21 January, off on a jaunt around the country from which he would not return until 6 February. Three days later at Twyford he was dancing naked with the Gibbings after which Moira Gibbings came to his bedroom for a "goodnight 'hug' ". As Gill records:

> "No intercourse or orgasm....just naked embracing and kissing and fondling for twenty minutes. Robert G. said he would not trust any other man on earth to enjoy such intimacy..."(D 24.1.25)

The next evening Gill pleasurably records 'Dear Mrs. G. nude.....lying in chair".

After such eroticized leisure Gill proceeded on a typically brisk and businesslike tour which included a visit to a Temple lawyer who was handling the wrangle with Hilary Pepler about Ditchling finance; a visit to Denis Tegetmeier who was eventually to be his son-in-law; a visit to Bradford to see Fr. John O'Connor, the translator of Maritain; a visit to the University of Birmingham to lecture on 'Art and Religion'; and a visit to Hawkesyard to see the Prior, Fr. Vincent McNabb.

During January William Rothenstein offered Gill a visiting professorship in wood-engraving and stone-carving at the Royal College of Art which Gill refused; he was out of sympathy with an establishment which taught that modern iniquity 'fine art',and he also doubted his capacity to remain aloof from the allure of the female students.

Dom Theodore Bailey was at Capel for two weeks in mid-February and after Gill's return they discussed, along with Philip

Hagreen and David Jones, the possibility of forming a confraternity of Catholic artists. Gill proposed that the charter should be translated into Latin by René Hague but Hagreen, whose misgivings about staying at Capel were increasing, was against the idea and David Jones was 'wavering'. Gill's desire for a guild could be read as a certain kind of insecurity although it is more profitable perhaps to read it rather as the desire to establish a mechanism to set standards that could determine the kind of artist suited to Gill's experiment. And certainly the remarkable homophonic similarity between 'Gill' and 'guild' suggests that the formation of such an apparently democratic structure did not necessarily have to threaten Gill's autocratic tendencies; Gill and guild sounded strangely synonymous. What is more, in the context of early twentieth century art, the foundation of groups (necessary in order to be noticed, remarked Ezra Pound) was almost *de rigeur*. But on this occasion, as the proposal was not greeted very warmly, Gill became petulant in the face of apathy, and maintained that the guild had already been founded by himself and Dom Theodore although thereafter the subject was hardly discussed. (MAC 201).

During February and March David Jones exhibited two works that he had painted during his short stay at Capel in a show at the LeFèvre Gallery entitled 'Pictures, Sculpture and Pottery by some British Artists Today' which included work by Ben and Winifred Nicholson and Edward Wolfe. On March 3 March Jones left Capel for Caldey Island where he would paint and engrave.

Caldey Island lies three miles from Tenby; its interior is relatively flat and rather uninspiring but its coast comprises sandy bays cupped by dangerous cliffs with many fissures, caves and blowholes. It is a smallish island measuring one and a half miles by three-quarters of a mile and the north part, facing Tenby, is of grey carboniferous limestone whereas the southern portion, below a line drawn from Sandtop to Drinkim bays, is of red sandstone. There are human remains and flint tools from as early as 8000 B.C. and the island has had monks living on it for the last 1500 years. The Welsh name *Ynys Byr* or *Ynys Pyr*, the Island of Pyro, is an eponym for the first Abbot who drowned himself one night in a drunken stupor. The English name derives from the Norse 'keld' — 'spring water' (with which the island is well served) and descends from the time that Vikings harried the south Wales coastline.

In 1136, only twenty-one years after Llanthony Priory was finished, the island was given to the Benedictine monks of Tiron in France and, like Llanthony, it fell victim several centuries later to the political ambitions of Henry VIII. The island developed as an important limestone quarry at the turn of the nineteenth century and one hundred years later, in 1906, Caldey was sold to an Anglican Benedictine brotherhood under Dom Aelred Carlyle. In 1913, as I have noted, these monks were received into the Roman Catholic Church but the years during which Eric Gill was at Capel-y-ffin were stormy ones for the Caldey monks, left in great debt after Dom Aelred's vast building programme. In fact in 1925 the ownership passed from the Benedictines who were nonetheless given a three year period in which to to rescue their financial situation. They could not do this and in September 1928, about the time that Gill moved from Capel, Caldey became a Cistercian foundation.

Jones went to Caldey on the suggestion of Philip Hagreen who had been convalescent there during the war and he was delighted with it. He gave the impression to William Blissett that the monastery was a "pretty hit-or-miss" affair (LC 21) and he found it a sympathetic place to work and an exciting place in which to paint. Jones later wrote:

> "It was in the Vale of Ewyas and on Caldey Island that I began to have some idea of what I personally would ask a painting to be, and I think from 1926 onwards there has been a fairly recognisable direction in my work"(DJL).

On 12 March Gill was off to London for three days to see Count Kessler, John Rothenstein, William Marchant of the Goupil Gallery and David Jones's work at the LeFèvre Gallery. It was during this visit that Gill suggested to Kessler that he might illustrate the *Ananga-Ranga* , the Indian love treatise, or "thirty four ways of doing it" as Gill remarked (SPE 166). Gill was endlessly fascinated by the erotic. Apart from the tracings of Indian erotica that Coomaraswamy sent to him, he collected newspaper clippings on subjects of aberrational sexual behaviour as well as on nudity and naturism. A scrapbook that he kept included not only photographs of the interesting dress of differ-

ent races and ecclesiastical garb but also a selection of photos of
women beginning to take their clothes off, photos of bathing cos-
tumes and lingerie including an advert that posed the question,
'Can woollies be dainty?' Also collected were some French
photos of *'Jeunes filles modernes'*, a picture of young girls in short
wide skirts, some nude women wrestling (shaven or retouched)
and a picture of a policeman, that guardian of morality, enjoying
a glimpse up the skirt of a fallen female demonstrator.

Mary Gill's birthday on 14 March drew Gill back to Capel
where he stayed only a few days, enjoying among other things a
concert and charades given by the children at the Attwaters. Despite Gill's affairs and sexual adventuring his marriage with Mary
Gill was clearly one of great mutual love. After one separation
Mary wrote to her husband of how "our bodies were so thankful
to lie together again" (November 1918 WAC) and when separated
they often sweetly appointed a particular time of night at which
they would each masturbate and thus be united in separation.

Gill left again for London on 19 March and during this visit
there is one diary entry which typifies Gill's enormous energy.
Given the fact that the London transport network of 1925 would
not have been so rapid though perhaps more efficient than our
own, and that during the course of the day he drew out two
inscriptions, Gill accomplished a phenomenal amount on the not
untypical 23 March:

> "To Mass 7.30 & Commn./ To Goupil Gallery/ to St. George's Hosp.
> & drew out inscript./ to A & N Stores re lettering/ to Ryl. N. Hosp.
> & drew out inscript. / to John Castle re. portrait / to Morley [the harp
> mender in South Kensington and not the suburb] re. Joanna's harp/
> to see Fr. McKee at the oratory/ back to D.T.'s 9.30'

After a weekend spent with Robert and Moira Gibbings discussing painting all day and reading Ellis's *Psychology of Sex* all
night, Gill returned to Capel on 27 March and worked on the
Kessler Vergil letters and on some bold and compelling lettering
for notices for the Army and Navy Stores in Victoria. For this
work Gill charged £22.19.00, significantly, with his strict atti-
tudes to just costing, not rounding it up. Another example of his
careful pricing is to be found in the estimate for a tablet to be
made in Portland or Capel-y-ffin stone for Lady Clarke a few
months later:

Stone	10.00	
Carr. [Carriage]	5.00	
Mason	15.00	
Letter Cutter	1.10.00	
Carr.	5.00	
E.G.'s fee	_3. 3.00_	
	£6. 8.00	
workshop_____	_1.12.00_	
	£8.00.00	(WAC)

Gill's fee is for drawing and all jobs carried a twenty-five per cent workshop charge.

In early April the family worked on the new Chapel which was blessed at 6 o'clock on the eleventh. This Chapel is still in use at the monastery and retains the rough and ready, 'no room at the inn' kind of feeling that it must have possessed in Gill's time. With a cold stone floor and simple white altar stone on which Jones's deteriorating tabernacle still stands, the Chapel houses loose pews for about ten people with space for six choristers. There are no windows on one side but from the other wall one can look out on to the brightness of the central garth. Dom Theodore graced the simple Chapel by lettering on the rafter and collar beam above the choir:

+ CHRISTVS + VINCIT. XTS. REGNAT + / CHRISTVS / IN SEM-
PITERNAM + IMPERAT+

and behind the altar:

+ PRO VNIVERSIS IMMOLATUS . DOMINVS. / + IPSE SACERDOS.
EXISTIT . ET. HOSTIA +.

As one passes out of the Chapel another work by Dom Theodore is still visible, a wall painting of St. Peter and Christ in a lightweight mock Byzantine style dominated by pale greens and yellows and painted in the year of the Chapel's sanctification. Passing out of the passage which leads from the Chapel through a mock gothic doorway one finds oneself on the outside steps of the monastery building facing the powerful mass of the Hatteral Ridge. It is the kind of landscape that, at least since the beginning of the Romantic era, has provided the mind with an image

3. The Chapel at Capel-y-ffin

for the power and pervasiveness of God.

In mid-April Gill was in London for four days, spending one night with Jones at Brockley and visiting the Goupil Gallery with which he was developing a secure relationship. William Marchant proposed that the gallery would take twenty-five per cent of whatever price Gill fixed on his sculptures though Marchant wrote that if he felt he "could get a bit more.....I should do so and we would divide equally between us the extra blood obtained from our victims" (WAC). Gill, in a forthcoming show, was to exhibit sculpture (including the *Sleeping Christ* in Caen stone) and drawings along with work by such artists as Sickert, Ginner and John. Later in the year, in October, a worldwide agency for wood engravings was established with a gallery commission of thirty-three and a third per cent and a sub-agency percentage for the Goupil of ten per cent over and above any sub-agent's commission, though Gill was allowed to continue to sell privately to personal friends.

Gill spent the rest of April and the early part of May at Capel. Laurie Cribb arrived to work with him just before the Hagreens, having decided that the Capel set-up was not congenial, left in early May. Cribb's brother Joseph had been Gill's first apprentice and Gill had been disappointed when Joseph decided not to live at Capel because his wife disliked the climate. However Laurie had also worked with Gill at Ditchling, liked the Black Mountains and, as he proved to be the finer craftsman, things turned out well. David Jones, in a letter to Harman Grisewood in 1970, noted that Laurie Cribb was a better inscription cutter than Gill himself and 'was *wholly* free of art-school aesthetics *and* from any awareness except that he was simply doing a job" (DG 228) — a stance that clearly reflected Gill's teaching. Like Jones himself however, Cribb could only work in a messy manner; David Kindersley remembered that he "drew out his inscriptions apparently without any certainty of where the letters should be and rubbed them out with spit and thumb. Carving eventually through a black mess of pencil lead, he produced sublime letter forms and spacing." (DK WAC).

Gordian, Gill's adopted son, who for his birthday on 10 May was given a pair of stilts that Gill himself had made, developed measles and congestion of the lung the very next day. A couple of weeks later Elizabeth and Joanna Gill came down with the illness though all were sufficiently recovered to bathe naked on several occasions at a nearby waterfall during the hot weather in the second week of June. During their illness Petra, leaving Mrs. Mairet's workshop at Ditchling, came to Capel-y-ffin for good. She would be a welcome addition; David Kindersley remarked that "she has always seemed...to be the calmest and most serene person that I've ever met" (CG/DK WAC).

Gill's relationship with each daughter was different in kind; as Cecil Gill summarized it:

> "Joan was closer to him intellectually....He could discuss points with her....he was more at home with Betty as regards practical affairs about the place, and I suppose he would delight in Petra as a place of repose"(CG/DKWAC).

MacCarthy suggests that any incestuous activity between Gill and his daughters does not appear to have harmed them (MAC 156) and otherwise Gill certainly appears to have been a caring father. In a letter to the girls when they were on pilgrimage to Rome Gill wrote that they were "the whole point" of his work: "Do you think we live how and where we do just because we like the view? No, but so that *you* may have a good chance" (15.7.25

WAC). For their part, there was obvious admiration for their father as a public man and an acceptance of his ways. Petra, when later asked whether she considered that Gill had been a good father, replied, "I think he was, yes" (BBC HRC) and Joanna remarked that "he has just coloured one's whole life without realising it" (BBC HRC).

Gill delivered the lettering for the Army and Navy Stores on 13 May when he next went to London. On this occasion he went to stay with Denis Tegetmeier in St. John's Wood. Tegetmeier, who had studied at the Central School of Arts and Crafts on an ex-serviceman's grant, as David Jones had done at Westminster, had refused an apprenticeship at Ditchling although he stayed there and helped from time to time. It was on this trip while walking across Hyde Park in the late evening on his way back to Tegetmeier's that Gill found the grass "dotted with 'lovers' " (D 14.5.25). Gill made a sketch and note of a dressed man reclining between the naked legs of a young woman on the back of an advert for a book about the construction of the locomotive *Caerphilly Castle*:

> "seen in Hyde Park (abt. 20 yds. from pathway) 14.5.25 10.0 p.m. summertime i.e. not quite dark. *Note well*: the couple were watched afterwards and were discovered to be quite obviously an ordinary couple of good middle class young people genuinely in love — he about 25-30, she abt. 20-25. He looked like a student or journalist — she like a girl in business. E.G." (MY 113).

Gill the sociologist and student of society is consorting amicably with Gill the voyeur.

In early June Gill received a playful letter from G.K. Chesterton trying to lure him into writing an article for *G.K.'s Weekly*; it seems that Gill was easily led because 'What's it all bloomin' well for?' appeared in the 20 June issue, followed by 'Art Appreciation' on 25 June. The former, as the title might suggest, is a typical example of the D.H. Lawrence vision of Gill the bumptious, "a tiresome uneducated workman arguing in a pub" (DHLP). However, in this particular case, Gill peppered his jaunty, spontaneous and colloquial article with some Latin. In a letter of 12 July, Desmond Chute took the author to task: "Is it good to drag in bits of Latin? Is not the problem of scholasticism today precisely the opposite — expressing old truths in new forms?" (12.7.25 WAC).

Once again, in mid-June, Gill was in London staying with Tegetmeier and sorting out passport problems in anticipation of his
daughter's forthcoming trip to Rome with Dr. John McQuillan, a
professor at St. Peter's College, Glasgow. On 18 June Gill met
David Jones at Paddington and they went off together to Waltham St Lawrence to visit Robert and Moira Gibbings. They
were joined by Fr. John O'Connor, Gill's confessor who, as Attwater notes, "probably appreciated and understood Eric better"
(CGL 63) than anybody else. Fr. O'Connor was a mixture of
"extensive and sometimes esoteric knowledge" (CGL 62) and unaffected Irish ebullience. He came to Waltham St Lawrence to
discuss the text which he was preparing for *The Song of Songs*
with the engraver Gill and the publisher Gibbings. The project is
not a surprising one for Fr. O'Connor seems to have shared
Gill's excessive interest in the erotic and his letters reveal a high
degree of interest in the positions and mechanics of love-making.

It seems that Gill didn't sleep very well when he was at Waltham St Lawrence; perhaps it was difficult to relax in a highly
erotic atmosphere where he had to remain unsatisfied. On the
two nights of this visit he was up very late talking with David
Jones about Petra to whom the young man had been engaged for
over a year.

The rest of June and the beginning of July passed quietly at
Capel. Gill in his *Autobiography* celebrated his "marvelous girls"
who managed

> "the baking and brewing and milking and butter-making, the twenty
> acres of farm...as well as all the housework, cooking and cleaning —
> and I, except perhaps in haymaking time, no help to anyone, unless
> you call keeping a general eye on the whole show helpful". (AUT
> 218-19)

David Jones arrived back at Capel on 10 July in good time to
taste Elizabeth's first brew of Capel beer sampled on the twelfth,
the day before Gill accompanied his daughters to Southampton
to send them off on the pilgrimage to Rome. He wrote a moving
letter to them while they were in Italy, describing how he
watched their boat pass out of sight:

> "...all three of you — all the children we have (all our eggs in one basket

— what a risk!) - all the fruit of love making (oh — there was great joy at your making — be sure of that!)....because you are the fruit of love (oh yes love, & not only lust, though there was on my part enough & to spare of that)..." (15.7.25 WAC).

Gill made use of the journey to make a swift round-trip to visit various members of his family and returned to Capel on 18 July.

Meanwhile the three girls had a very good voyage on the SS Tabanan and disembarked at Marseilles after which they had a more troublesome journey to Rome, missing a connection at Genoa and eventually arriving in Rome at midnight. On the train they had "enormous lunch bags" and couldn't persuade Petra to take wine or brandy against her sickness (EG 24.7.25 WAC). Joanna Gill wrote that on arrival "we were simply filthy and dead tired and Petra was sick, everyone was quite cheerful all the same, except one girl and she just fell on her bed and cried she was so tired" (24.7.25 WAC). Gill's "lovely long letter" was there to greet them on arrival and their suite at the Hotel D'Italy was large and comfortable. They made two visits to St. John Lateran and Joanna found the Coliseum "perfectly wonderful" and St. Peter's "beyond words" but the heat in July was disturbing. Joanna records, with a candour that she can only have learnt from her father, that after lunch the girls took hot baths and "lay on our beds with hardly anything on" (24.7.25 WAC).

The relationship between René Hague and Joanna Gill had obviously developed because Gill, possibly taking advantage of his daughter's absence, spent a whole morning discussing her with Hague. Later, on the evening of the same day, he discussed the young man's prospects as Hague, with his quick wit and lively mind, was clearly feeling restless in the rôle of agricultural labourer.

After almost a month at Capel in which he and Eric Gill had enjoyed many long walks together, Jones left on 5 August for Caldey Island, returning to Capel with Fr. Prior a week later. While he was away the girls returned from their pilgrimage to Rome and Gill recorded that they were "all very well" (D 7.8.25).

During the previous months Gill had been engaged on many small diverse projects but by the end of July he had begun serious work on *The Song of Songs* which occupied him almost constantly until early October. While steady work continued on that project there was much walking, a birthday party for Petra on 18 August and visitors including Robert and Moira Gibbings at the end of the month. Haymaking occupied the early part of September and after much intense work on *The Song of Songs*, Gill was off to Birmingham on the 25th. From there he travelled to Waltham St Lawrence for four days of collaborative work on the printing of *The Song of Songs*, taking one night off to visit G.K. Chesterton at nearby Beaconsfield.

Dom Theodore Bailey was at Capel-y-ffin at this time and one day he and Gill and Petra and David Jones went sketching up the Hay valley. On the next day Gill began a debate with Dom Theodore and David Jones on the subject of *'id quod visum placet'*, the source of Gill's pamphlet of that name.

We must not make the mistake of thinking that life at Capel was, for David Jones, all work and debate and no play. René Hague remembers an occasion when Jones drove the milk float to Llanvihangel to meet Petra and found it difficult "to force the obstinate pony, Jessie, into a smart trot, even though he stood up like an ancient charioteer and urged her on with loud cries and sharp blows from the slack of the reigns" (DG 33). This image of Jones as an "ancient charioteer" is no doubt one that would have appealed to him, especially as he entertained a lifelong and unrealized ambition to ride a horse.

Jones, who had been born in Brockley, Kent, had felt from a very early age the 'Welsh thing' to be close to his heart. Such deep affection and sense of belonging gave this south-east Londoner a place in the heart of "genuine Taffies" like actor Richard Burton who read the part of John Ball in one of Douglas Cleverdon's radio productions of *In Parenthesis*. Jones was one of the three great Welshmen of the century, according to Burton, who considered his own performance in the radio production of *In Parenthesis* to be the finest thing he had done in his long and varied career. Burton was clearly affected by Jones's writing; in 1968, describing the beauties of his wife Elizabeth Taylor in his private notebooks, Burton called her "clement and loving, Dulcis Imperatrix", a formulation familiar to readers of *In Parenthesis* (p.81).

A crucifix which Gill had been intermittently carving since June was packed on 6 October, the same day that he began carving a "girl with hair" (D 6.10.25) in Capel-y-ffin stone. While

Jones stayed on in Wales, Gill took the crucifix to London and stayed with his daughter Joanna at Jones's parents in Brockley. When Gill returned on the 16 October Jones was ready to leave; it is interesting to note this for it shows that both men led independent working lives that dictated individual rhythms and patterns. They were drawn together by friendship and common principles but there is no question of discipleship binding the younger man.

For Gill another trip to London followed swiftly in which he saw a lot of Denis Tegetmeier and made a visit to Stanley Morison at the Monotype Corporation. To a mechanical engineer who worked there Gill did not appear at all like a famous artist and in a comment that would have much pleased Gill, the man observed that "you'd have said he was a good mechanic — or anyway some good workman who knew his job!" (MR 41 3 1958). Gill also saw a lot of David Jones who accompanied him to Waltham St Lawrence where there was the inevitable nude dancing in the evening. It is difficult to imagine David Jones participating in this kind of activity or, for that matter, in the naked bathing and general atmosphere of heightened sexuality that surrounded Gill.

Returning home on 30 October, Gill agreed to decide either to rent the Grange, the large house adjacent to the monastery buildings, for £60 a year or to buy it outright for £1200. This was a daring consideration for the family was, at this time, very hard up; as Gill put it in a letter to his sister Enid Clay, thanking her for a welcome cheque for the engravings for *Sonnets and Verses*, he had "various works on hand not bringing in cash until they're finished" and because of the "fearful expense of repairs" (October 1925 WAC) at Capel during the previous year it was difficult to make ends meet. Gill's net income after expenses had dipped severely from nearly £1500 in 1923 to about £400 in 1924, the year of the troubled and expensive move to Capel. In 1925 this grew to £659 and it stayed at around this mark until it rose dramatically to £1355 in 1928, the year of the move to Piggotts.

Denis Tegetmeier visited Capel and there were evening debates with him and Dom Theodore and René Hague. The upshot of the recent debate on the subject of '*id quod visum placet*' was that after a short trip to Dorset and Bristol between 7 and 16 November, Gill dictated an essay on this subject to Elizabeth Bill, his secretary and mistress in residence. The essay was to be published by Gibbings at The Golden Cockerel Press but not under that imprint as it was based too heavily on Catholic doctrine to suit the non-ecumenical nature of the press.

In mid-November Gill began drawing alphabets for Stanley Morison. He also read 'The Rime of the Ancient Mariner' to the children, the poem that was to be the inspiration for a series of copper engravings that Jones made during 1928 and 1929. What Gill chose to read to the children often had a backward-looking or nostalgic style or form, for instance Malory, Edmund Spenser or Coleridge's ballads.

Back in London at the end of the month, Gill visited the Passport Office in anticipation of the projected pilgrimage to Rome that the adults were to undertake over Christmas. Gill also visited the Redfern Gallery in connection with the Society of Wood Engravers Exhibition and his trip ended at Waltham St Lawrence where after supper and nude dancing on the 30 November Robert and Moira Gibbings "fucked one another.....M. holding me the while" (D. 30.11.25). Significantly, David Jones arrived the next day and Gill's diary entry records a more sober activity for that evening, the discussion of "b ooks etc." (D. p.1.12.25). Perhaps this registers Jones's relationship to the more liberal antics in which Gill engaged.

In early December Gill stayed at Capel involved with sundry activities but on the nineteenth he went to London and took his wife, on the following day, to meet the Joneses at Brockley. The trip to Rome was to be started at 7 p.m. on the next day at Victoria Station when the Gills met Donald Attwater, Elizabeth Bill and the other pilgrims. As the train passed them at 9.20, members of the Ditchling community waved because, among other things, Gill was off to visit that beloved ex-member of the community Desmond Chute. At Newhaven they embarked for Dieppe and Gill took dinner on the boat with Donald Attwater. The next day they spent travelling and arrived at Genoa at 8 a.m. on 22 December where Chute and Gill had only two hours of talk before the train left for Rome. Gill recorded in his diary:

"Passed Pisa about 2.0 a most lovely afternoon & a most lovely sight of the city and river — more beautiful than I had ever imagined... arr. Rome 11.0 & drove in taxis to Ospizia Santa Marta. To bed at midnight — immediately under the shadow of St. Peter's" (D. 22.12.25).

The next three days were largely taken up by hearing Mass in various churches and by attending a Papal Audience and address to the pilgrims in the *Sala Ducale*.

Meanwhile back at Capel it was very cold and five inches of snow covered everything; Petra Gill, writing to her parents, declared that "We shall think about you all on Christmas day dear Mother and Daddy, we miss you very much" (WAC).

Gill had visited Rome before in 1907 "to see the inscriptions" (Letter 15.7.25 WAC) but on this occasion there was only time on Christmas Day itself for limited sightseeing. The group left the city before dawn on 26 December and after a rough crossing reached Capel-y-ffin in good time to see in the New Year. But is it not perhaps significant to note that the second Christmas of the Capel period was spent away from home?

6. Eric Gill: Drawing, Sculpture and Typography

Drawing

A good deal of Eric Gill's drawing is indifferent and about it there is not a lot that one should say. Often we find a hard, over-precise and uninflected quality in his line which reveals a suspicious lack of uncertainty; as David Jones put it, "there is evidence of the linear, and of the lyrical — not so much of the observed, for he was too concerned with concepts" (E&A 294). And with Gill the claims that he made for art, while they intellectually elucidate the processes, are often in excess of his own sensitivity to a particular medium. Roger Fry, on receipt of a drawing in January 1912, perceptively remarked that the figure drawn was possessed of a "rather mean and trivial elegance", going on to adjure Gill "to avoid prettiness like the devil" and that the drawing in question had come "perilously near to prettiness" (Letter 25.1.12 WAC); would that Gill had followed Fry's advice.

In the Introduction to Douglas Cleverdon's 1929 book of Gill engravings, the artist wrote that as a younger man,

> "apart from about a fortnight in the Life Class at the L.C.C. Central School when I was about 20 and a day's drawing from a model in 1910, I never drew from life at all except at home..." (EEG 1929).

But in May 1926 Gill spent thirteen days in Paris drawing at the Grand Chaumière, often with Robert Gibbings; it is during this brief period Gill claims that he consciously did life drawing for the first time in his life. With the exceptions noted above, he had hitherto only been concerned with the figure in occasional sketches (e.g. 'Moira Gibbings nude' 30.11.24), in engravings and in sculpture. While John Rothenstein noted in his Introduction to the posthumously published *First Nudes* of 1926 (publ. 1954), "both in outlook and by his want of early training Gill was unfitted for direct drawing of the naked model", Gill himself maintained that a late start in this discipline had certain advantages:

> "If you are going to draw from the naked model at all the best time to do it is rather late in life, when the experience of living has fulfilled the mind and given a deeper, more sensual as well as more spiritual meaning to material things" (25N 1).

But do these qualities manifest themselves in Gill's drawing? Rothenstein was blunt in his criticism of the first nudes which perhaps had been better left unpublished: "Regarded simply as drawings from life they are less accomplished than numbers produced each year in art schools" (FN). He felt that most of the drawings were "slight" and, strangely for a stone carver and sculptor, most were "hardly more than two dimensional representations" (FN). Gill's emphasis on line rather than bulk was, however, a deliberate choice; in some miscellaneous notes on 'Drawing' written in 1927 Gill stated that "the substance of a drawing is line....Bad drawing...is the use of lines without consideration of the idea of contour. Bad drawing is drawing deprived of understanding — it is insensitive" (WAC). Now how does that relate to Gill's own achievement?

While an attempt at sensuality is apparent in most of Gill's life drawing, sensitivity is notably absent. More often than not, Gill's nudes are self-offering objects of delectation, the figments of male fantasies. Sensuous curves, the erogenous zones and more particularly the pubic area, are given prominence while fingers, feet and even faces, those windows onto the soul, are ignored or relegated by a clumsy and ill-drawn shorthand. The psychology of the person or their relation to the world is neglected in the titillating isolation of these figures.

In a letter to Desmond Chute of October and November 1928, Gill contended that "the male's enjoyment of woman actual or imaginary is in itself...foreign to art" (WAC). While art is preoccupied with formal problems it is cavalier, as we have seen, to suggest that these remain independent of emotional considerations. Gill himself sensed this when he wrote in his *Autobiography* "that sheer sensuality has not often succeeded in hiding under a camouflage of intellectual purity" (AUT 227n.). It is a problem that we come up against time and time again with Gill; he sought to restrain his lasciviousness, he sought to camouflage the overwhelming nature of his eroticism and the result is a coy or sheepish naughtiness. It is in his private, unpublished erotica, when he brings sensuality and sensitivity into an honest relation with the strongest drives of his personality, that he achieves some worthwhile drawing.

Certainly in the drawings made during the first session at the Chaumière the line is often unexpressively hard and the faces when drawn are drawn badly. While art presents a formal rather than a descriptive problem, no serious and worthwhile artist would become involved in abstracted formal questions before resolving and consolidating some contactual facts. It is true that many of the poses and viewpoints of the *First Nudes* are inventive but the sketches were obviously made rapidly and as a result the drawing of the inexperienced Gill is often catastrophic. If he had drawn with a softer pencil these nudes might have appeared more subtle; we are left with the ubiquitous slick line, facile shading and sloppy and insufficiently observed drawing. They are altogether symptomatic of a criticism that is often levelled at Gill, which is that at any one time he never appeared "prepared for second thoughts or a third thought" (BBC HRC). When, as in the drawing made at Oliver Lodge's studio in London a little later in the year, Gill does seem to have considered the mood and personality of the model, the resulting drawing is of a finer order.

But there is not only the question of generally sloppy drawing but of a certain tastelessness in various conventions that Gill adopts. From a later visit to the Chaumière in May 1928 there is one drawing in which the face displays a silly ecstasy and in which the pudendum and nipples seem to have been almost machine-tooled. The effect is such that the artist appears to be delineating a sexual target. And not only is the quality of the line generally slick but an unfortunate shading, particularly in the later drawings, occurs intermittently along the outside contours of the body that gives a rather vulgar, glowing effect to the drawing.

However, as I have hinted, among the unpublished erotica there is occasionally to be found a greater degree of integrity and, despite the explicit nature of the subject, a greater propriety. Of

5. Unpublished Drawing, Couple Lovemaking

4. Life drawing at Oliver Lodge's, 5.10.1926

course there are some indulgent fantasies of big-breasted, small-waisted women with swirling hair. Furthermore, the women tend to beach themselves on the penis unsupported by anything else — presumably to convey a sense of maximum pleasure. The *reductio ad absurdum* of such a pose is the drawing for a voluptuous sculpture of a woman supported by a huge plinth in the shape of a mammoth penis that fills the space between her legs. There are quick, slick sketches of coitus, mutual masturbation, and even more extravagent fantasies such as a dog with an erection coming up to lick a woman's genitals. There is a fantastic Poseidon/Merman with genitals bulging between his twin tails. And there is typical Gill schoolboyishness; he cut from a magazine: "Joke of the Week: 'When is a whole less than a whole?' 'When it's apart' " and stuck it beneath a cartoon he drew of a striding woman pointing to the separated lips of her reddened vagina. One silly decorative watercolour called 'First Love (or the Boy Scouts and the girl guides)' shows a girl sitting in a boy's lap with her leg raised and as his erect penis searches about her pudendum her hand directs his exploration. But also among these drawings there is to be found a sensitive enjoyment of the beauty of the subject matter. One such is the tight organization of a formalized couple in which the man bends over the woman to lick her. There is no date on this energetically scribbled work but on the back there is a quick animal line drawing by David Jones which looks as if it might have been drawn towards the end of the Capel or early Pigotts period. Gill wished his little sketch to act as a visual manifesto; below the drawing he wrote "Man is matter and spirit — both real and both good". There are works, like this cunnilingual couple, which while not being devoid of Gillian mannerisms do have a refreshing vigour. There is an energetic drawing in blue and red crayon, now in the British Museum, of a reclining man masturbating; this has a vital, all-over energy that Gill does not usually allow himself. Also in the British Museum is a drawing scribbled in pencil where the figure appears to embrace his organ in a tenderly loving pose.

The bound volume of thirty-nine erotic items in the Clark Library, along with scattered items elsewhere, reveals a rich variety of styles. As Coomaraswamy sent Gill Indian erotica that tradition has been absorbed. There is a watercolour celebration of lovemaking in a light, pleasingly decorative manner that is spiked

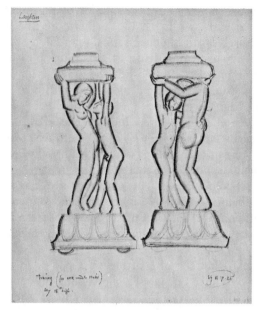

6. Designs for candlesticks

7. "Man is matter and spirit: both real and both good" — unpublished
drawing

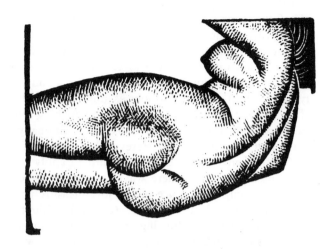

8. 'Woman', 1926, experiment with multiple tool

9. Unpublished drawing

by its title, 'Lot's Daughter'; it has, however, none of the obscenity of the young Cézanne's treatment of the same theme in which we witness the rapinous advantage that the old man takes of his daughter's enthusiasm. Gill's version rather allows the soft receiving cushion into which the lovers sink to act as a sensuous metaphor for the pleasure of coitus; another version by Gill with Lot lying flat on flattened cushions is unremarkable by comparison. The stylized drawing of a couple love-making which I have chosen to reproduce on page 64 is as compositionally refined as any work that Gill published. Here was a subject of which Gill was sufficiently enamoured to compel him to apply the inventive aspect of his artistic skills; here was the attempt to render under the form of pencil, the essence of the joy, pleasure and beauty of coitus. Another sketch I reproduce (p.67), by adopting a more casual and naïve style of drawing, reveals something of the male wonder at his excitement at the prospect of joining with a woman — it is a wonder that was keenly experienced by Gill. So privately, Gill felt no need to compromise, gloss over, nor, in the best examples, to play the naughty boy. Here was a man possessed of certain plastic skills putting these to the service of celebrating one of the most exquisite human joys.

Gill, of course, made a number of drawings during this period that were neither life drawings nor erotica. As a stone carver, one function of drawing in Gill's life was in the preparation of designs for cut or carved works. In July 1925 Gill produced two intriguing designs for oak candlesticks (p.65) which clearly demonstrate that Gill's carving talents and particular manner of stylization might well have suited him for a grand career in the decorative arts. Gill's drawing seems ultimately insensitive when it merely concerns itself with line. The slight suggestion of sculptural form or bodily mass in the designs for these candlesticks, enhances his powers of expression in a two-dimensional medium. And surely this is predictable in the drawing of a stone carver who possessed a heightened awareness of the tactile joy of volume.

A drawing made in 1928 of Mary Gill knitting evokes an almost eerie combination of homeliness and mechanical precision. Compared with a loving drawing that David Jones made of the same subject in the same three-quarter profile in pencil and crayon five years earlier, it lacks delicacy. Gill made his drawing in Salies-de-Béarn and describes it in his diaries as "a bad likeness". The expression that he captures, however, does have a kind of cheekiness or knowingness which is commensurate with the obvious warmth and sexuality of their relationship. Earlier in the very same day Gill had drawn chairs and tables at Lousteau's café in the *place*. Here the casual atmosphere of the café is echoed by the relaxed handling of the line and the organization of the forms is refreshingly almost haphazard. It is one of Gill's most engaging drawings. He left behind his often useful tendency towards architectural exactitude, reserving that for more suitable subjects like St. Vincent's, the local church where the family heard Mass. But although *At Lousteau's* is above average because of a certain relaxation, the pencil is too hard and the paper of too poor a quality to elicit the finest drawing.

During this period Gill also drew street scenes in Paris, the chimney of a ruined cottage in the Ewyas Valley, the *Villa des Palmiers* in Salies, but unless he was drawing the body, more often than not he drew in order to design. Of all the media in which Eric Gill worked, drawings made for their own sake were usually among the least compelling of his artefacts; perhaps the lack of utility of such drawing was ultimately unsympathetic to a man who was at his best when he was at his most practical.

Sculpture

Occasioned to a certain extent by the sudden interest in primitive artefacture, carving again became a common sculptural procedure at the beginning of the twentieth century. Along with artists like Epstein, Gaudier-Brzeska, Brancusi, Modigliani and Henry Moore, Gill carved directly from the block. The fact that he was formally less exciting than the aforementioned resulted from the fact that he tended to work formulaically. The sensitive *Times Literary Supplement* reviewer of Rothenstein's *Eric Gill* of 1927 remarked that, "Formality being a matter of duty rather than of inclination or sensibility, Mr Gill conceives intellectually of a hieratic art, which admits little sensibility, since the idea of the work of art is in the artist's mind, composed and ready" (TLS 7.7.27). The reviewer goes on to note that this was dangerous as "the intellect cannot always conceive of formal relations which come very easily to a natural or trained sensibility". These remarks were obviously inspired by Rothenstein's point that Gill was an artist whose work was dominated by the "intellect rather than" by his "aesthetic sensibility" (REG).

David Jones noted that Gill "conceived in relief rather than in the round even when the work was technically 'in the round' " (E&A 292), going on to explain that "the four sides of a block of stone were each worked rather as separate faces and so contrived as to 'join up' satisfactorily — rather than growing organically from the centre of the block, as seems to happen in true 'in the round' sculpture" and that this resulted, sometimes, in a "feeling of toyishness and a lack of weight and volume" (E&A 292). Jones found in Gill's sculpture all the faults that can be discerned in his drawing and engraving: a mannered quality, a slickness and a striving for the logically finished work. Jones cherished Gill for his incidental stone artefacts such as a water-stoup rather than for his more self-conscious sculptures.

Gill had made an early and strong impact on the fine-art world with a one-man show at the Chenil Gallery in January 1911. Wyndham Lewis had called Gill's sculpture "small, excellent and ribald" (RC EG AD) and Lewis is not renowned for the generosity of his praise. This debut was somewhat consolidated when Roger Fry included eight pieces by Gill in the Second Post-Impressionist Exhibition of 1912. The twenty-one year old Mark Gertler wrote to William Rothenstein that he found Gill's sculptures "most *inspiringly* beautiful! Really splendid. I wish you would tell him so. I could have wept for joy!...When I went out the world seemed full of pleasure and joy and I was happy all that night" (WAC). Fry, writing to Gill after the exhibition, declared that "Your reputation and future success seem to me assured" (5.11.12 WAC). But thereafter Gill did not develop in a direction that was in sympathy with the major trends in modern art. He didn't carve "big and blunt" as Fry wished (Let 25.1.12 WAC). The "weight and volume" which Jones found lacking in Gill are major preoccupations of early twentieth-century stone sculpting. The forms of Epstein, Dobson and Moore are bulky, squat quasi-primitive forms and Gill's tendency was towards linearity and grace. Above all, Gill's Christian subject-matter was out of step with the spirit of the age.

David Jones's honest, balanced and insighted assessment, privileged by close acquaintance and proximity, is invaluable in elucidating Gill's disjunctive relation with the world in which he lived. Gill

> "sought to work as though a culture of some sort existed or, at all events, he worked as though one should, and could *make* a culture exist. Because of his singular qualities as a man he sometimes achieved carvings that looked something like the products of true culture" (E&A 289).

In Jones's Spenglerian perception of culture and civilization as distinct entities, the former is "the organism born of Mother Earth" and the latter is a "mechanism proceeding from hardened fabric"; in a culture a person lives inwardly whereas in a civilization a person lives "outwards...amongst 'facts' " (OS DW I 353). Now Gill, because he had the misfortune to live in a "civilizational phase", could only find it impossible to express the soul of a culture; the problem is not one of mere artistry but that Gill was foredoomed by having the misfortune to live "in a period devoid of culture" (E&A 291). While Gill maintained along with Coomaraswamy that "every man was a special kind of artist" he found in actual fact that he as an artist was an oddity, "a special kind of man", because of the nature of the modern world in which he worked. Spengler noted that the person who lives in a civilizational phase "is irreligious....Bitterly as he may feel the inner emptiness and poverty, earnestly as he may long to be religious it is out of his power to be so" (OS DW I 409). It is in part as a result of such a dislocation between desire and possibility that Gill's work seems to be at odds with his age. Jones's contextualising of Gill's accomplishments and deficiencies in a wider civilization context of course derives ultimately from Gill's own philosophical example and this is one reason that Jones legitimately credits Gill with "singular qualities as a man"; Gill's great gift was to discuss, to develop and disseminate ideas either verbally, through his writings or through certain of his plastic works. The works themselves might be flawed but the support system of thoughts that stood behind them were, more often than not, sound.

Apart from Jones's perceptions about the dessication of culture and apart from the problems of overt Christian expression in twentieth century art, the other problem that compromised some of Gill's work was as we have already observed, his insatiable sexuality. There are explicitly sexual sculptures, such as the bas-relief *Lovers* now in the Clark Library at the University of California, Los Angeles, which have a simplicity untainted by mannerism or affectation. There is an honest delight in the arrangement of the forms and a celebration of a moment of human joy. But in other cases the naughty schoolboy all too easily asserts himself. One of Gill's motives for making sculpture was, as he records in his *Autobiography*, his "erotical exuberance" (121). When he writes of a sculpture of a "naked young woman" he notes that

> "if I hadn't very much wanted a naked young woman, I don't think I should ever have done it. Lord how exciting! — and not merely touching her but actually making her" (AUT 159).

Gill, the voyeur, indulges his phallocratic power.

If we make the somewhat unfair comparison between an erotic work like *Splits No. 2* (made in the year before Gill moved to Capel) and a work by Rodin such as *Iris, Messenger of the Gods*, we can see that Rodin's piece, despite the effrontery of its flagrant pose, exhibits a feeling for the musculature of the whole and for the spirit of its subject. It is clearly not an excuse, as with Gill's pose, for vaginal delectation. Both men were sensual but Rodin subordinated his interest in certain aspects of the female anatomy to larger concerns. Compare the flexible and supple positions of Rodin's spontaneous dance studies of 1910 with the stiffness of most Gill nudes and we can clearly perceive the gulf that separates these artists.

The problem with carving at Capel was transportation. It was difficult enough to get human beings up to the monastery let alone huge and heavy lumps of stone. This resulted in a number of small carvings being made during this period and eventually necessitated the taking of a studio in London in 1927.

A small sculpture called *Deposition* in Hoptonwood stone was one of Gill's first works made after the move to Capel. Hoptonwood stone is an oolitic limestone full of shell fossils and there are consequent variations in its hardness so care is needed when working with it (*viz* DK WAC). Speaight noted that Philip Hagreen, who spent days with Gill rubbing and eventually french-polishing the sculpture to achieve a sheen, observed that the fact that it was a nude presented problems; those who wanted a Deposition would not want a nude and vice versa (SPE 154). But apart from the small wound from the spear thrust does the sculpture assert its subject matter? The small carving remained Gill's own favourite amongst his sculptures but its elegantly flowing form dissolves unfortunately into a somewhat cloying sweetness.

The face of *The Sleeping Christ* carved in Caen stone in late February and early March of 1925 has, in the clean cut expertise of the delineating chisel, a kind of facile mannersism. Likewise the bas-relief, *Girl with Hair* carved in the difficult Capel-y-ffin stone which was begun in October 1925 but not finished until March of the following year, has, paradoxically, an almost machined effect, despite Gill's decision to allow the roughness of the stone to express the textured effect of the hair. Even the apparently odd positioning of the girl's left forearm, her abundant hair, or her restrained yet evident sexuality do not rescue this carving from mediocrity.

Gill had the habit of adding colour to sculptures; a crucifix which he was carving in the summer of 1925 in Portland stone has painted hair, wounds and loincloth. This sculpture (in HRC) is over-fussy in its total effect and the realistic tension of a body hanging from nailed hands is at odds with the decorative quality of the crown of thorns, the gently flowing hair, and the neatly ordered loin cloth.

A *Carytid* carved in 1927 in Wellingtonia Pine (WAC), more than usually chunky and Moore-like, is one of Gill's few carvings in wood. This stocky figure with its awkward self-embrace is more psychologically suggestive than is usual with Gill's work and yet it lacks the tension of an early Dobson or Moore.

During the winter of 1927, while Gill was in the south of France, Laurie Cribb started carving away the oak background of what was to become the Rossall School Memorial. Gill had submitted designs for this project in January, June and August of the previous year, and the design which had been at once accomplished was merely subjected to a series of simple modifications. In this bas-relief there is considerable organizational skill in the arrangement of the scene of the crucifixion. On either side of the central group of worshippers the two thieves react gesturally to scenes from the life of John the Baptist that form the outer panels of the triptych. The thief on the left, while he is turned away

ABSENTES ADSUNT

10. The Rossall School Memorial

74

from the Baptism of Christ by John and is beholding Christ crucified nonetheless has his hands upraised as if he too is receiving some kind of blessing from heaven. The thief on the right recoils from the beheading of the Baptist. While one thief looks towards heaven, the other beholds a kind of hell.

It was at his Chelsea studio where Gill spent about six months towards the end of the Capel period that he was able to undertake larger works of sculpture. It was there that his sister Angela modelled for the large Hoptonwood sculpture that came to be known as *Mankind*. Although in the late 1970s Malcolm Yorke had to track this sculpture down to the "Tate Gallery's store on an industrial estate in North Acton" (MY 225), it having been neither unwrapped nor exhibited for years, it had been much celebrated when first exhibited at the Goupil Gallery in 1928. The *Daily Mail*, whose readership Gill held in slight regard, and which two years before had purchased for the nation another now forgotten tribute to woman, Dod Proctor's *Morning*, was enthusiastic about *Mankind*. The *Times* reviewer was, however, more sagacious: "For a work of its size it relies a little too much on the intrinsic beauty of the subject" (1.3.28). Robert Gibbings, who visited almost daily while Gill was working on this sculpture and who suggested that the figure should be kneeling to ease the line of the thigh as it met the supporting base, wrote in detail about the sculpture's evolution:

> "I saw the great column of stone, some eight or nine feet high, he told me then that his only idea about it was to carve the largest female torso that he could get out of the stone. He said he didn't want to be bothered with head, arms and legs, he just wanted to enjoy carving a body which would represent his ideal of feminine beauty....Under his instructions then, his mason worked until he himself took over with hammer and punch. Soon it was possible to see the rough outline of the huge figure. Then the punch gave way to the claw which was to carry it all a stage further, in readiness for the final carving with the chisel. I remember that, in his eagerness to see some part of the stone finished, he went ahead with the chisel before he had finished all over with the claw, so that at one time there were three different states to be seen: the deep ridges, encircling the forms, from the punch, the 'combed' surface from the claw, and the smooth stone almost polished by his amazing skill with the chisel....It was like undressing a girl, he said, each layer of stone a garment, first one got rid of the rough woollies...finally the delicate silk. Eric liked these little innocent naughtinesses." (RG CDW 81)

Well these "naughtinesses" appear to have stunted Gill's creative intelligence and sensitivity; significantly Gill wasn't 'bothered" with the limbs, only the sexualized core of the body.

The *Times* reviewer pointed out that Gill tended to use indigenous stone such as Hoptonwood, Portland, Bath or Beer and mistakenly suggested that his "native talent in native materials...can hold its own with anything in Europe" (1.3.28). While England has consistently made an important contribution to sculpture in the twentieth century it is doubtful whether Gill himself has contributed anything of international importance. Gill celebrated the courage of the cubists and the post-impressionists in their search for form but does not seem to have taken up that search himself. He side-stepped modernism and never found a pertinent equivalent for the religious art of an earlier period. It is more as a technician that we should praise Gill, though being a technician carried with it certain problems; as Speaight put it, Gill "believed in too many rules and he thought that all one had to do was to follow them" (SPE 228). However, Jones notes that Gill's pre-eminence 'as a stone-cutter, as a master of his trade, is admitted by all sculptors, whatever they may think of his aesthetic" (E&A 291).

Typography

One area of visual expression in which Gill's contribution is unquestionably of great and possibly lasting importance is in the designing of type faces. Gill had been associated with lettering in one way or another since his youth. He had been a student of and had lodged with Edward Johnston the author of the seminal book *Writing & Illuminating & Lettering* which contained a chapter on inscriptional stone-cutting by Gill who had swiftly made a reputation in that medium. Apart from much inscriptional letter-cutting which provided a constant source of income throughout his life, Gill also became involved in the engravings of initial letters for titles and headings which were used by Count Kessler at his Cranach Press and by Robert Gibbings at The Golden Cockerel Press. Some of these are possessed of the virtues of clarity and rationality but others are rendered illegible by the complexity of their decorative invention. Such confusion exists in the often praised capital letters for the *Four Gospels* (1931). For example, in 'Then the soldiers of the Governor' the design is so cluttered that the word "Then" is absolutely illegible.

What we are concerned with here however is typography, and that differs from lettering. Typography is the design of legible and easy-to-read letter forms that can be used in any combination without any modification of the individual forms. As Stanley Morison put it, "Typography is the efficient means to an essentially utilitarian and only accidentally aesthetic end..." (FL 8). While Gill refused to have electrotypes made of the initials that he had designed for the Cranach Press, he did, in this period when he was living at Capel at the furthest remove from industrial civilization, compromise with industry and, in his work with Stanley Morison of the Lanston Monotype Corporation, participate in the industrial procedures of mechanical typography.

In 1924 Gill declined Morison's invitation to contribute to the typographic journal *The Fleuron*, declaring that "typography is not my line of country" (BW WAC). But very soon afterwards Gill became involved with the Monotype Corporation and Beatrice Warde perceived in Gill's attitude a "growing respect and interest" in the related technical problems (BW WAC). If typography involved machines and 'machine-facture' at least it was a utile and democratic art. In its capacity to bring the rational and good to the eyes of many, it was closer to Gill's ideals than the 'Arts and Crafts' type production of expensive books on expensive paper for private presses such as The Golden Cockerel. Gill's dislike of industry was that it reduced people "to a sub-human condition of intellectual irresponsibility" but he noted that "it doesn't follow that all industrial products are bad *things*" (LET 295). Typography was one way in which art and industry, beauty and mass production could join hands to bring a goodness to the widest possible public.

By late November 1925, Gill had been persuaded by Stanley Morison of the Monotype Corporation to produce some drawings for a proposed typeface that would derive from the stone carved alphabet. Although begun before Gill's *Sans Serif* this did not make its first public appearance till 1929 in *The Fleuron* where it was used for Walter Shewring's translation of *The Passion of Perpetua and Felicity* and accordingly the type became

ABCDEFGHIJKLMNO
PQRSTUVWWXYZabcde
fghijklmnopqrstuvwwxyz

ABDEGHJKMNQRS
TUVWXYZabcdefgh
ijklmnopqrstuvwwxyz

11. *Perpetua* and *Sans Serif* Type

known as *Perpetua* and the italic form as *Felicity*. Gill wrote an accompanying note for the first appearance of his designs. The type was

> "cut by the Lanston Monotype Corporation from drawings and alphabets made by me. These drawings were not made with special reference to typography — they were simply letters, drawn with brush and ink. For the typographical quality of the fount, as also for the remarkably fine and precise cutting of the punches, the Monotype Corporation is to be praised. In my opinion 'Perpetua' is commendable in that, in spite of many distinctive characters, it retains that commonplaceness and normality which is essential to a good book-type"(FL).

The collaborative process had begun successfully and the designs clearly pleased Stanley Morison who had been convinced of Gill's potential as a type designer: "They are creations. There was never anything of that kind before Gill did this, and never has been anything since. The capitals that he did, I think, will be immortal. They'll be used as long as the Roman alphabet is used anywhere" (SM&EG BC 32 I). This is high praise coming from the man who Douglas Cleverdon credits as being mainly responsible for the "typographical renaissance of the 1920s" (DC EEG 15). Robert Harling considers *Perpetua* to be "undoubtedly the finest classical alphabet evolved in this country between the eras of *Caslon* and *Baskerville* and our own time, with the possible exception of *Bell*" (RH LF 48). In the opinion of Roy Brewer, '*Perpetua* combines the grace and presence of inscriptional roman with the robust appearance which is needed to give a type 'colour' on the book page". He notes that it was the "first classic roman typeface to be designed specifically for machine composition" (EGMWLL 45 & 47) and this meant, as Beatrice Warde has noted, that there was "no need to brace serifs against the crushing and unevenly balanced weight of the old hand press" (FL 8 46). Consequently the serifs could retain the qualities of elegance and refinement that marked the fact that they had been designed by one skilled in the deft termination of a Roman form incised in stone.

The evolution of this type was clearly of seminal importance in Gill's subsequent type designing. Gill's *Golden Cockerel* type is described by Harling as "essentially an expanded and rounded version of *Perpetua*" (RH LF 51) and the *Joanna* type for the Hague and Gill press at Pigotts is also related. Furthermore, in the matter of typography it seems that Gill was prepared to allow himself the time to have second thoughts; two years after *Perpetua* first appeared Gill was still worrying with the form of the lower case y. In a letter to Stanley Morison, Gill suggested that the current "dotty y" was "out of keeping with the form" (15.4.31 WAC). He drew six new versions of which he recommended the square cut serif on the descender, the form eventually adopted.

On 30 October 1926 Gill was in Bristol where he lettered the signboard for Douglas Cleverdon's bookshop in Park Street. During this visit, Gill spent some days in bed with the 'flu and whilst recuperating he passed his time drawing out alphabets. As Cleverdon recalls:

> "A few months later Morison was staying with us for the week-end in the studio above the bookshop. He much admired both the fascia and the lettering in the blank book and while we were contemplating and discussing the latter, the idea emerged that E.G. should be commissioned to do a sans for Monotype" (RH LF 44).

Morison attributed the need for a current *sans serif* type face to the growing industrialization of life and the increasingly intense competition that was developing in the commercial world. Laurie Cribb had resorted to such bold letter forms on notice-boards at Capel-y-ffin "to warn off the hundreds of visitors who persisted in coming to see the monastery and Father Ignatius' grave" (AUT 219). In flight from the publicity of Ditchling, Gill indignantly recorded the impertinence of these tourists: "They would walk in without asking and you would find them wandering in and out of your bedrooms. And when you asked them what...they were doing, they would say: Can we see a monk?"

The examples of Gill's *sans serif* which had caught Morison's attention derived from the alphabet that Edward Johnston had designed for the London Underground in 1916. Gill developed this design which, as Beatrice Warde noted , had been contrived "in proud conformity to the canons of the Roman alphabet" and "intelligently... paraphrased" Johnston's forms (BW WAC).

What is now known as *Gill Sans* (like *Perpetua* and the italic form *Felicity*) is the joint achievement of Gill, Morison and the typecutters of the Monotype Corporation. Harling usefully illustrates how the designers in the Type Drawing Office modified the *Gill Sans* designs. He illustrates the type before and after the modifications of Morison, Burch, Pierpoint and Steltzer. Not only did these square Gill's slanting cut-offs to the ascenders and descenders of the b d p and q characters but also closed the space between the top and bottom bowls of the lower case g and reduced the height of the interior of the lower bowl which resulted in a tighter and more elegant letter.

Gill Sans seems, in many ways, more successful than Paul Renner's *Futura sans serif* design which appeared in Germany in 1927. Renner's lower case g may appear to be more modern at first sight but its bowl rests in an unhappy, top-heavy relation to the curve of the descender and Gill's less obtrusive dots for his i and j seem less affected. While Gill's capitals owe much to Johnston, the Q and R possess a grace which Johnston's and certainly Renner's lack.

Gill Sans was greeted with disdain at a trade conference in 1928 but it proved to be acceptable to the public. While it was the job of the serif to guide the eye across the page in a continuous and lengthy passage, the *sans serif* is declamatory and ideal for notices. Gill's own is, according to Harling, "the most reasonable and readable" (RH LF 44) of all those that have been produced. Furthermore the upper case forms, being of uniform thickness,are patient of altered size and weight without upsetting distortion. Gill had produced a fool-proof mechanical type that was ironically suited to the increasingly blunt communications of an accelerating commercialized society.

It was in his final year at Capel that Gill was beginning to think of the *Golden Cockerel* typeface on which he worked seriously in 1929, having first produced *Solus*. He went on, during the following seven years, to design *Joanna, Aries, Jubilee* and *Bunyan*. Gill's association with the Monotype Corporation was to provide a steady and increasing source of income. In 1926 Gill received a cheque from Morison for £30 in initial payment for *Perpetua*. In September of the following year he received £5 for the initial drawings for *Gill Sans*. In the spring of 1928 he began to receive a biannual retaining fee of £52.10.00 from the Monotype Corporation. So by 1936, when the annual fee went up to £200, he had earned, independently of the fees for actual designs, nearly £1000 from his association with the corporation.

The letter is the best example of what the neo-Thomists considered to be the *sine qua non* of the work of art, that it is not a representation of a thing but the thing itself. As a letter is the thing and not the picture of a thing, a pure beauty, rational and without extraneous connotation could be achieved. Gill could, as Denis Tegetmeier noted, be concerned "to unearth, so to speak, what constitutes the A-ness of the A, the B-ness of the B" (RH LF 31). The artist is able, with the letter, to address purely formal problems, and while the personality will exert its influence on the choices made, it would be unlikely in the designing of a functional type to overmaster the enterprise. (In Gill's case one might say, 'A-ness' could be sought without the complicating overtones of 'Anus'.) Gill was at his best when he was the commissioned workman; he was right to fear "art-nonsense" for he was uneasy in the realmof art. The thing about a letter which is unlike a drawing, sculpture or engraving is that you can get a letter right.

7. 1926 'In a dying land'

Because Christmas had been spent in Rome it was only at the beginning of January that Gill printed his engraved versions of the Christmas cards designed by each of his three girls. The design done by Joanna, the youngest, was linear and a little severe, perhaps somewhat surprisingly for the most ebullient of Gill's children. Petra's *Child in Manger* was both rougher and gutsier with chortling animals at the edge, on either side of the crib. Elizabeth, the eldest, produced a more sophisticated design in which Mary bends to offer the Christ-child her breast. The clean lines of this composition were complicated by the addition of cross-hatching and two haloes when the card was printed by the intaglio process. Gill obviously took these engravings seriously because he included some of the children's designs in Douglas Cleverdon's 1929 edition of his engravings. It also seems that Mary Gill participated in these activites; there is a dry-point attributed to her of a rather mournful Madonna with a tiny child surrounded by energetic foliage.

During the second week of January Gill began some commissioned engraving work for a Passion Book which he continued after a brief but busy trip to London between 21 and 26 January. In London he met David Jones at a meeting of the Society of Wood Engravers and went on with him to an Arts and Crafts Exhibition afterwards. Although Gill was critical of the paradoxically exclusive markets of the Arts and Crafts movement he had to acknowledge an affinity with their methods and with certain of their aims.

At this time Gill was troubled by the fact that René Hague felt unable to go on with Chapel Farm. Gill had put £100 into the venture so when Hague, who didn't wish to face many years of penury, left on 5 February, Gill was understandably disappointed.

The question of whether to rent or to buy the Grange remained unresolved and one of its occupants, Fr. Joseph, was sufficiently unwell at the beginning of February for there to be no Mass celebrated at the monastery for two weeks. But, despite these upsets, Gill was working hard engraving and his sexual experimen - tation continued; he recorded in his diary that for the first time he practiced the still method:

> "i.e. the man keeps quite still and stiff inside his wife while she comes 2 or 3 times and then he comes at the end. Very beautiful method" (D 24.2.26).

Towards the end of February, Gill made a quick journey to London. He lunched with Dom Theodore Bailey and David Jones and afterwards went to Waltham St Lawrence with René Hague to discuss 'various affairs"with Robert Gibbings. During his peri- ods away from Capel, Gill was obviously content to seek out the company of those who were, on other occasions, frequent and long-term visitors to the monastery. What was important at Capel was the practice of arts in a sympathetic environment and to a certain extent that environment was created and controlled by the constant discussion between like-minded people. How good it was if necessary trips to London to visit galleries or to dis- charge business could be embellished by similar discussion and it is a measure of the friendship between Jones and Gill to note how frequently they were happy to see one another when Gill was in the capital.

At the beginning of March Gill was finishing the carving of a nude in Capel-y-ffin stone, despatching drawings for a show at the Goupil Gallery and drawing and engraving an illustration for *Id Quod Visum Placet* which was to be printed in a limited edition of 150 copies at the Golden Cockerel Press.

Gill's relationship with his secretary, Elizabeth Bill, was clearly exuberant at this time. On 20 March she was measuring his penis with a foot rule ("down and up" — D 20.3.26) and he spent the afternoon of 21 March singing with her. Penis-measuring was a preoccupation; in the British Museum there is another example done in September of the following year and a psychologist who was shown some of Gill's erotica observed that he was not only a highly sexed man but that he must have had "a particular phallic fixation" (SPE 179). There are indeed endless studies of penises in various states and styles. One such study to be found in the British Museum and done in March 1923 with "foreskin pulled back" presents an almost reptilian smoothness contrived in the style of the closely graded shading of a Victorian etching. Gill certainly exhibited the male's capacity to be proud of his own powers of tumescence and he was also fascinated by semen. No doubt Elizabeth Bill, with her tastes for faintly pornographic books (MAC 205), was interested, later in the year, when Gill showed her slides of semen under a microscope. And perhaps it was in connection with these adventures or perhaps in connection with his artistic endeavours that during February Gill took delivery of two dozen "of our 18/- per doz. series of Art Studies" from the curiously named Robespierre and Pinaud, a modelling agency and vendors of life studies who operated from the discreet address: Flat 2, No. 7 Colville Gdns, Bayswater. Perhaps these inspired some curvacious and exuberant pencil drawings with coloured nipples done "from photos" on 22 February when Gill returned from London. In any case, on that particular date Gill should be indulged; it was, after all, his birthday.

At the end of April Gill took his first trip to Salies-de-Béarn with his daughter Petra and Elizabeth Bill. After sitting up the night with Miss Bill in the Salon of the cross-channel ferry they arrived in Paris in the very early morning and took a taxi to the Hotel de l'Europe off the Place St. Michel where Robert Gibbings was staying. They were in Paris for two days before taking the overnight train from the old Gare D'Orsay to the Pays Basque.

Gill wrote to Desmond Chute on 5 May:

> "Miss Bill...is buying a small property here at Salies and, as we intend to share it with her, we thought it good to come and inspect with her before she actually settled on it." (LET 210).

Gill evidently approved of the eight roomed *Villa des Palmiers* because a couple of days later Elizabeth Bill was at the *notaire's* engaged in the process of buying it. Gill was also delighted by the old town which, as he stated in his *Autobiography* , had "a quality of goodness and quietness and even holiness which seems to have gone forever from England" (230). Another passage in the *Auto-*

biography shows quite clearly that he was under no illusions about Salies:

> "Was it not 'run' by its local politicians? Had it not got one of the worst possible memorials of 'the Great War'?..Was there not the hideous half-built hotel — the building abandoned because the 'company' went bankrupt? Was not the parish church almost falling down?" (234).

While the countryside around Salies and the old town itself was steeped in the past, the more modern part was given over to a spa that was popular in the early part of this century. Its thermal waters were reputed to be particularly efficacious for gynecological disorders and the railway poster that advertised fashionable Salies a few years earlier had displayed a semi-nude woman blooming with its benefits. While Gill might have enjoyed the unashamed frankness of this advertisement, a second version, one with covered breasts, had to be produced to satisfy the propriety of the town itself.

Salies was thriving; it functioned as a normal town whereas Capel and the countryside around had the air of "a dying land — unspoiled but dying" (AUT 229). Many Welshmen who returned from the First World War had found themselves not only changed by their experiences but found that modern civilization had made inroads into their country, inroads exacerbated by petrol, the cinema and broadcasting. The result was that many of these young men gravitated towards the towns. Gill, lamenting this situation, spoke sadly of the "twenty ruined cottages between Capel-y-ffin and Llanthony four miles lower down the valley" (AUT 229). The situation afforded yet another opportunity for Gill to rail against the prevailing economic structure:

> "The population of the valley was but a quarter of what it had been fifty years before....The young men had gone to the mines and were wandering unemployed in the Rhondda, their fathers could not call them home for the city of London found it more profitable to foster Australian Capitalist sheep farming than to preserve the thousand-year traditions of the South Wales mountains" (AUT 229).

What is more, while Gill, Petra and Elizabeth Bill were in Salies, the General Strike started. Gill wondered, in a letter to Desmond Chute, what the outcome would be and asked, "Is there one single leader on either side who sees that a civilization is judged by its products & not by its social conditions?" (LET 210).

In the five days of this first visit to Salies Gill sketched the *Villa des Palmiers*, labelling the peach, palm, and eucalyptus trees in the garden. He also sketched in the town and even did some carving. From nearby Sauveterre, which Gill found "most splendid" (D 7.5.26), he had his first glimpse of the Pyrenees. Gill was obviously very happy; tea one day consisted of "goose and wine" enjoyed at a "most beautiful farm" with a "most beautiful family" (D 6.5.26). Gill found the scene to be "a grand example of human life in all its vigour and feebleness, its joy and pathos" (AUT 236).

Back in Paris, Gill had a very full schedule. On 9 May, after two Masses in Notre Dame, he took lunch with Robert and Moira Gibbings and spent the afternoon looking at modern French art in the Louvre. After writing a lecture back in his room at the Hotel de l'Europe he went to the *Folies Bergères* to see the nineteen year old Josephine Baker who only eight months before had created a furore in the *Revue Nègre*. Baker was famous for slapping her buttocks in tempo to 'Yes, Sir, That's My Baby', and her bare-breasted mating dance brought audiences to the point of frenzy; one can only suppose that Gill was no exception as, on a later trip to Paris, he enjoyed particularly the dancing scenes in a film about Africa. Colette called Josephine Baker "a most beautiful panther" and Anita Loos spoke of her "witty rear end".

The following morning, which was his adopted son Gordian's birthday, Gill attended Mass at the church of St. Severin, only two minutes walk from the Hotel de l'Europe. This intimate church, which became a favourite for Gill, was built on the site of a Merovingian necropolis. In the thirteenth century it was a centre for university meetings before being burnt down and rebuilt around 1450, at the height of the Gothic period. Its dark interior and cloister gardens offer a quiet retreat from the crowded alleys and small busy streets of the left bank. The rest of that morning was spent with Elizabeth Bill in unsuccessful attempts to interest art dealers in acting as an agency for wood engravings and the afternoon was spent with Robert Gibbings drawing at the *Academie Chaumière*.

On 11 May, with Petra, Elizabeth Bill and Robert and Moira Gibbings, Gill spent "a fine day" at Chartres. On the following morning Gill made a successful arrangement with an art dealer to act as a French agent but later on the same day he left his portfolio of prints in a taxi. Nonetheless, he drew again at the Chaumière in the afternoon as he did on the three following days and found that he was enjoying life drawing "v. much" (P/C to MG 11.5.26 WAC).

On 13 May Gill visited the studio of the sculptor Ossip Zadkine off the Rue D'Assas. However much, later in life, Zadkine sought the angular, agitated, trembling line, producing literally overwrought works, during the twenties he sculpted torsos which have an affinity with Gill's manner of calm simplicity. There is, of course, in Zadkine's work of this period, evidence of the influence of cubism, of such diverse artists as Modigliani and Archipenko, but while he is more eclectic than Gill, his work like Gill's veers between the good and the ghastly.

Late one night, after Petra had gone to bed, the adults "visited a strange place of which R.G. had been given the address and saw some girls nude posturing in lascivious manners" (D 15.5.26). This is entered in the Diaries immediately after Gill recorded a meeting with Jacques Maritain at the Catholic Institute in the Rue Vaugirard. To see such diverse realms juxtaposed (even though the events themselves took place on different days) is emblematic of the diverse tendencies in Gill's life.

During this visit to Paris Gill also made an ephemeral visual work which was as inventive as it was fun. He painted a face on Robert Gibbings's chest, using nipples for eyes and the navel as a mouth when he helped the Gibbings's dress for a party at Juliano's.

After a second visit to the Préfecture about the missing portfolio, Gill returned on 17 May, to London. While Petra went to Brockley to see David Jones, Gill went to meet René Hague at Waltham St Lawrence. On 19 May he was back at Capel for nine days, correcting the proofs of *Id Quod Visum Placet* and moving into a new mason's shop.

Gill was off to Paris once again on 28 May, this time with his daughter Elizabeth and Elizabeth Bill who was bound for Salies-de-Béarn. Gill recovered the missing portfolio that he had left in the taxi, drew again at the Chaumière and saw a good deal of Zadkine. He also visited Aristide Maillol at Marly-le-Roi and there made a drawing of a dancing couple in a refreshingly loose style; the girl was naked, the man wore a loincloth and clutched her breast.

Elizabeth Gill's twenty-first birthday occurred on 1 June and father and daughter visited the Eiffel Tower. Gill had refused to sanction her engagement to David Pepler until she came of age and though she had spent a lot of time visiting him at Ditchling it had not been possible to pass beyond the point of intention until this date. Surely enough, the day after they returned to Capel on 10 June David Pepler came for a visit. In a letter to the Reverend Rope, Gill wrote that "Betty is engaged to David Pepler. He is a good and steady young man — but oh how we wish that it may not entangle her with...Hilarian chess moves!" (4.9. 26 WAC). Gill's mother wrote to her son later in the year that Elizabeth was "a dear girl. I expect, after all, she has instinctively done the best for herself in becoming engaged to the man she knows so well" (14.11.26 WAC).

Gill read Joyce's *Portrait of the Artist as a Young Man* in three days, doubtless fascinated by its invocation of St. Thomas's three conditions pertaining to beauty: proportion, integrity and clarity (PAYM 218). A short while later Gill spent a day reading Chaucer's *Troilus and Criseyde,* prior to a weekend visit of Robert and Moira Gibbings in early July to discuss a possible engraved edition of that work.

On 12 July Gill was off to Bristol to begin fixing a relief sculpture in Highbury Chapel. He stayed with the mother of his old friend, Desmond Chute. Although Chute was by this time much enjoying not only the beneficent weather but also the exciting political climate of Italy in the mid 1920s, he had been temporarily 'recalled' to visit his apparently domineering mother and so Gill had the pleasure of his company. Cecil Gill recalled Chute as

"a 'Beardsley' type of figure. Rather long and graceful, swathed about with shawls....He always felt the cold. He had tuberculosis in early life and it left him with tubercular iritis, which was a terrible thing for a visual artist."

Cecil Gill noted that between his brother and Chute there existed "a deep personal attachment....Desmond himself said that he loved Eric — and he was more than a brother, you might say. He had the sort of devotion for Eric of a lover" (CG/DK WAC).

For the next few days Gill was on the move, visiting the Epstein show in London and visiting Waltham St Lawrence to discuss *Troilus and Criseyde* and René Hague's future with Robert Gibbings. Hague's position was somewhat uncertain at this time. Gill wrote to Joanna who was enjoying herself in London that Hague's prospects with the Golden Cockerel Press were by no means certain. Gill the possessive father was also gently intransigent on a more personal subject: "So, my darling Joan, it's up to you to give him the 'tip' & not let him take the future for granted — either as regards *you* or as regards the G. Cockerel". But while there was obvious tension between Hague and Gill, the latter obviously had no mean opinion of the young man's qualities: "By the bye, why doesn't René *write* [I mean write a book or essays]...do reviewing for the Cath. Times!" (7.7.26 WAC).

On 15 July Gill was back in Bristol where he continued to fix the statue at Highbury Chapel. During this visit he began to spend a lot of time with the young Douglas Cleverdon who had just opened up as a bookseller. Cleverdon's premises in Park Street had become a meeting place for the Bristol intelligentsia and the Clifton Arts Club met on the first floor above the shop.

Gill returned to Capel on 19 July and stayed there until 9 August. During this period he began drawing and engraving some of the blocks for *Troilus and Criseyde*. Except for short visits to London, Bristol and Waltham St Lawrence Gill spent August and most of September at Capel where the population was in a state of constant flux; among the visitors were René Hague, David Pepler, Denis Tegetmeier, David Jones, Fr. Gray and Fr. Prior. While people like Denis Tegetmeier helped Gill with the hay harvest, Jones with his reluctance to do very much about the place, set to work on the drawing and watercolour *Mr. Gill's Hay Harvest* which has often been reproduced and which suggests something of the undeliberate but undeniably quasi-medieval quality of life at Capel. I say "undeliberate" because, as Speaight notes (SPE 231), Gill was upset when Maritain, visiting Pigotts in 1932, found the workshop just like the middle ages.

John Rothenstein came for a visit of nine days on 11 September, the day that David Jones left for London. Rothenstein recalls that he enjoyed "every instant" of his visit. Despite the constant rain, the damp house, the lack of hot water, lack of newspapers and "spartan food", he found that Gill's "sharp-edged genial talk warmed the bleak house" (JR SL 127). Rothenstein also recalled elsewhere the "dark eyes" of the departing Jones which had "in their depths a little touch of fanaticism" and his "anonymous" dress that contrasted sharply with Gill's "black biretta, rough black cassock gathered in at the waist, black stockings cross-gartered, and sandals"(JR MEP 1-M 289). After Jones's departure, Gill remarked to Rothenstein that "he's a jolly good artist" and that "a lot will be heard of him before long".

David Jones, the south-east Londoner who stuck solidly by his Welsh descent, 'Dai Greatcoat' to his friends, 'Dafydd Jones' on the signature of certain paintings and letters, spent, during these years as an intermittent visitor to Capel and Caldey, more time in Wales than during the rest of his long life. He spent this time in Wales in closed, essentially English establishments but it is certain that this painter and poet-to-be who would later conjure the fantastic worlds of Welsh history and mythology was deeply affected by the landscape about Capel; as he was to put it in *The Roman Quarry*, "the deepest thing outcrops on the highest hill" (RQ38). The experience of this landscape would be both inspiration and consolation to a man who didn't much like to move about and who came to venerate 'site', 'place' and rooted culture and yet who spent most of his life as a nomad, either living with friends or in residential hotels in places as historically unevocative as Sidmouth, Harrow or Kensington and Chelsea. Of course, even in unlikely situations Jones would usually contrive an historic association. A door on a typical south-coast sun-porch becomes *Manawydan's Glass Door* as Jones looks through it towards the French coast and ponders the memories "of all the evils they had ever sustained" during the First World War (MAB Guest 46-7/IP Prol). Likewise, a painting of an anonymous hill in Northumberland is invested with historical significance by its title, *The Legion's Ridge*. Even if such a link appears tenuous it is better that it has been made, as paintings of St John's Wood High Street or of people promenading in Sidmouth which do not venture such connections appear, by comparison, disappointingly flimsy.

The setting of any one of the poems that David Jones would write from 1928 onwards frequently dissolves spatially and temporally and yet, more often than not, the bulk of the work remains rooted in a particular and historically charged site. As with the trenches, experienced between 1915 and 1918 and which became the subject of a writing made between 1928 and 1932, one of these anchors was the south Welsh border uplands, experienced during his visits to the Ewyas valley between 1924 and 1928 and written about in different 'fragments' of poems from the early 1940s until his death in 1974. But for the fact of this time at Capel the Wales which Jones imagined during these later decades could have been put together from the comfort of any reasonable library. In later life, Jones inhabited the world of his reading, plundering the literary, mythological and historical traditions which were biographically meaningful to him. Jones's 'Wales', like his 'Jerusalem' or 'Rome' or 'London', is largely a *bricolage* of intellectually assimilated elements envigorated by the unique music of his diction. Had it not been for the contactual experience of the south Welsh borders this vision might have been in danger of becoming fanciful or otherwise parched by learning. Likewise, if Jones had not boiled tea or cleaned latrines in the trenches it is doubtful whether *In Parenthesis*'s cast of historical extras such as Arthur or Artaxerxes would have possessed the kind of vitality and credibility requisite to great writing. It is the grandeur of vision salted by the common touch that puts Jones's poetry in a league above countless versifiers such as Charles Williams who dabbled in the backwaters of increasingly impertinent mythology. The best of Jones's poetry has a kind of Poundian smack, a requisite "now-ness" (E&A 209) which the Americans and the Irish often achieve but which the English, if they attempt something grand, often lack. Dylan Thomas recorded 'Dai's Boast' for a radio production of *In Parenthesis*, pages of high-flown, mythologically charged poetry, with a cigarette hanging from his mouth. The image is emblematic of Jones's range.

So the months which Jones spent looking at the borderlands in order to paint and draw his increasingly supple landscapes, imbued his vision of a mythological Wales, formulated decades later, with a contactual vitality. Jones's personal experience of the area would echo and ramify in 'Mabinog's Liturgy' in *The Anathemata*, in 'The Sleeping Lord' and in passages in *The Roman Quarry*. If Eric Gill showed little sign of taking any visual influence from any particular locality whatsoever, physical contact with Wales was very important for Jones. Gill's phallocraticism drove on obliviously whereas Jones was receptive to the terrain of the marches. It might, in fact, be tempting to perceive in the embosoming rotundities of this landscape a contributory stimulus for Jones's implementation of the concept of the "feminine principle", This concept itself appears to be one of the least satisfactory of Jones's dichotomous distinctions. It subsists on outmoded, male-determined archetypes and in a world blessed by the refreshing explorations of feminism, seems retrogressive. While perhaps not as damaging as Gill's pervasive phallocraticism, Jones's "feminine principle" remains, among other things, a less than satisfactory metaphor for the creative mode. But in relation to Jones's experience of the border uplands, it is not so much the rotund hills of South Wales "embosoming" the bardic tradition but rather the hardness of this resistant terrain which is evident in Jones's later poetry. While he believed that in the very origins of Celtdom there was a matriarchal tradition ('*Y Mamau*'), he also acknowledged a 'duality'; on the one side there were indeed Mother Goddesses but on the other side, "the chariot-fighting, champion-fighting, gold-wearing warrior aristocracy" (NLW 1978 Dep V/12 17 — crossed through). So rather than pondering a clumsy gender metaphor it is better to consider this terrain in relation to its rooted and complex culture, Jones's version of which is a mixture of literary, mythological and historical material. Let us glance at this complex amalgam for a moment.

The south Wales landscape is seen by Jones as none other than the Sleeping Lord himself, a mythical *rex quondam rexque futurus* whom the Welsh await as their saviour. While the figure possesses healing and restorative qualities and affinities with Christ, he is also an embodiment of Welsh military prowess, a kind of Llywelyn. This Sleeping Lord *is* Wales and certainly the geophysical reality of the country has been, to some extent, its saviour. Language and culture have been preserved by a forbidding terrain that deters invaders:

> His unconforming bed, as yet
> is by the muses kept.
> And shall be, so these Welshmen say, till the thick rotundities give
> (ANA p.68).

Jones uses the difficult terrain and unremitting harshness of the climate to temper his celebration of the subtlety and strangeness of Welsh culture. The weather itself is used as an expressive image for the peculiar quality of the Welsh native imagination:

> their very elements
> refract their thoughts — their brain-pans are as full of mist
> as their hill-circles.
>
> (*RQ* p.5).

But the climate also reflects the strength and hardness of the place; it is often seen as threatening or unsettling:

> Tawny-black sky-scurries
> low over
> Ysgyryd hill
>
> (*SL* p.90).

Wales has triumphed over political humiliation through its literature of incredible delicacy and complexity. As others before him, Jones associates the Welsh in this respect with the Trojans from whom they were traditionally descended through the figure of Brutus who gave our island its name. This association was ancient; a history written about 1282, that terminal year for Welsh Princes, celebrated the early inhabitants as "Trojan debris swept into the wooded savagery of Cambria". Jones indeed marked this passage in his copy of Powicke's *The Thirteenth Century 1216-1307* (NLW p 383). Reflecting this sense of defeat and diaspora, Jones mused that

> in the broken
> *tir y blaenau*
> these broken dregs of Troea
> yet again muster
> (*SL* p.95).

They "muster" and preserve ancient traditions. The descendants of Brutus, the Bret-Wealas, as Jones noted, "alone of the peoples of this island arose from within the Western Xtian imperium" (DJ PW 8 3 7). This places the Welsh, not on the periphery of western Europe, but in the mainstream of Classical Christian European tradition.

Wales is viewed by Jones as having been ravaged by orogenic upheaval, uncompromising weather and by the invading Romans and Irish. It has been traversed by warring mobile armies, politically subdued by the English and latterly exploited by the alien plutocrats of whom Gill was disposed to talk. The mythological creature which Jones used to express the wasting of this land was that damaging incarnation of evil, the boar *Twrch Trwyth*. The course of this beast's rampage as described in 'Culhwch and Olwen' in *The Mabinogion* was once plotted by Jones on a quarter inch Ordnance Survey Map of South Wales (NLW). The tusks of this hog

> have stove in
> the wattled walls of the white dwellings
> (*SL* p.90)

and thus Jones calls this country the "hog-wasted *blaendir* ", translating *"blaendir"* in his footnotes as "hill country" and "place of boundaries".

So while Eric Gill used the ideal *modus vivendi* of a secluded situation to bluntly denounce technocratic civilisation, Jones came to utilize a complex of the historical and mythological culture of the Welsh underpinned by the terrain and climate as a potent order which opposed the "civilisational", utilitarian age of "Roman hardness" which his revered Oswald Spengler (JM 36-64) defined as our inheritance (OS 1 26, 30, 44). The dichotomy is between a rooted culture which adheres to and expresses its own site and a cosmocratic power that plunders and reduces everything to a common level, between the ethos explored in Jones's 'The Tutelar of the Place' and that in 'The Tribune's Visitation'. It is, in fact, a sophistication of a Gillian dichotomy and if Jones's discussion and friendship with Gill sowed the intellectual seeds of such dichotomous thinking then his time with Gill in the Welsh mountains also gave him the experiential, observed reality through which he could view and control his received historical and mythological matter. And Jones further sophisticated this complex into what became an extended metaphor for the creative mode itself. The mythology, terrain and climate are all characterized by metamorphosis. As poetry exists by virtue of the suggestively transformative possibilities of language, Jones has thus found the perfect vehicle for celebrating the makerly mode. As well as portraying a rooted culture Jones also provides us with a vision of a possible manner of seeing and interpreting the world. The key to Jones's imagined Wales which evokes the creative mode itself is that "ceaseless metamorphosis" is "the only constant" (*RQ* p 35).

But all this is to look ahead decades. Jones, whose first 'attempt' at extended writing (*In Parenthesis*) was found by T.S. Eliot to be "a work of genius" (*IP* vii), whose second 'attempt' (*The Anathemata*) was found by W.H. Auden to be the greatest long poem in English made during the twentieth century, had by the time of his visits to Wales written nothing more than a couple of propagandistic and intensely patriotic essays from the trenches. What is more, during this period of his visits to Capel-y-ffin Jones was pre-occupied with the visual arts, with the subtle inflexions of the engraver's tool and the nuances of form, light and atmosphere in the surrounding landscape, transmuting all that into the medium of watercolour, transubstantiating the border uplands "under the form of" paint.

From the point of view of Gill's career the most important visitor to Capel at this time was Douglas Cleverdon who was driven to Wales by Desmond Chute. Cleverdon, like Rothenstein, found the monastery "bleak, dark and dank" but found Gill himself, with his "twinkling eyes.....very friendly and good humoured and responsive"(DC EEG xiv). Gill and Cleverdon spent much time walking together during the two weeks of the visit and they decided that the bookseller should act as a Bristol agent for the engravings. On one occasion Gill was writing invoices for *Id Quod Visum Placet* and suggested that Cleverdon, as a bookseller, should actually be engaged in this task. Cleverdon accordingly took over the distribution of the pamphlet and this paved the way for his decision to publish *Art and Love* in 1927. The growing friendship between the two men was also significant inasmuch as Cleverdon became one of Gill's favourite male models and there are drawings of Cleverdon in the British Museum that Gill made on the last evening of this visit. Desmond Chute, for his part, wrote to Gill that he returned from his visit to Capel "cheered, clarified, reconstituted, enriched..." (P/C 20.9.26 GLE).

Gill was engaged on a sculpture in Portland stone of lovers with their arms round each other's necks and, upon finishing it, he started carving in Caen stone a head of Mary Magdalene which took only six days to complete. On 24 September Gill went to Waltham St Lawrence to discuss *Troilus*. From there he went to

London where he saw a lot of David Jones and returned home via
Bristol. The death of an aunt took him away from Capel only two
days after his return and, apart from one week between 15 and 22
October, the month was spent in London or Bristol. During this
week spent at home Gill was working on *Troilus* and reading
Joyce's *Dubliners* from which he progressed to *Ulysses* which he
started reading in Bristol when he stayed there to work on Douglas Cleverdon's shop signboard, that proto form of Gill *Sans
Serif*. Coming down with the 'flu gave Gill some time in bed
during which he occupied himself by drawing out experimental
letter designs. Whilst Gill was recuperating, the often ailing Desmond Chute drew his "beloved Master" swathed in an armchair
and with a deep and almost devilish cleft in the middle of his
brow.

Joanna Gill left Capel with Elizabeth Bill in early October to
travel to Salies-de-Béarn. Miss Bill was going to supervise the
renovation of the *Villa des Palmiers* and Joanna, which is remarkable for a girl of sixteen, accompanied her to share the task of
reconnoitring the town. In Salies they stayed with Mr Ansted,
the father of Elizabeth Bill's son, at the *Villa Cubaine*.
Joanna found this Mr Ansted "quite small...rather old and dodery
(sic), but very good fun, and very fond of Elizabeth" (LMG 10.
10. 26 WAC).

A plasterer, painter and gardener began almost at once to work
on the Villa but in this respect Mr Ansted was "rather a bore". He

> keeps telling Elizabeth what he would do if it were *his* house, and he
> is so keen on beating the people down in their prices, if I were
> Elizabeth I should scream sometimes, but still he is an awful dear too
> (JGLEG 28.10.26 WAC).

In a letter to her sister Petra we get more intimate details. Mr
Ansted was always "hugging" Miss Bill

> and holding her hand, and when we are out he holds her arm. He is
> often talking about what he and Elizabeth used to do, and about the
> people they met here 16 years ago, it is quite misterrious (sic)'
> (18.10.26 WAC).

Ansted's presence as old lover and husband-to-be was one with
which Gill would have to contend during his time at Salies.

The scouts found a room in the old town that would be suitable for Gill's work. They found a priest to educate Gordian. They began making curtains at a furious rate. They visited the Hagreens who had moved to the south of France and were living close to Lourdes and Joanna found them "both much better and more cheerful" (LMG 11.12.26 WAC). Madame Lousteau at the café in the *place* was "awfully nice, she often talks to me, she always admires Petra's things, especially my cloak, she is a perfect dear" (JGEMG 12.11.26 WAC). Joanna had her ears pierced which "didn't hurt very much really" but it made her "feel a bit wonkey" (JGEMG 19.11.26 WAC) and she bought a pair of plain gold earrings to go in them. She advised the family that

> it will be cheaper in the end if we have a bonne at first, you see in the market they all speak Patois and if you can't they know you are English, and put all the prices up and you have to bargain like anything' (JGEMG 19.11.26 WAC).

Work was temporarily halted on the villa by bad weather but by mid-December Joanna was writing anxiously that she hoped "it won't be too stiff and tidy, it seems so frightfully bran [sic] new and clean now" (JGEG 11.12.26 WAC).

Meanwhile, back at Capel-y-ffin, the first snow had fallen as early as the end of October; Gill wrote to his daughter who was "basking in the sun":

> You remember — snow — small white stuff, rain really only colder — you know cold; that is, you know, not *hot* — opposite of hot — have to wear extra clothes — more clothes — thicker ones — wool — better to be married than single — warmer in bed' (23.10.26 WAC).

Gill spent most of November at Capel engraving. The ailing Fr. Joseph moved into the monastery and the Attwaters moved into the Grange where they had a house-warming party. Copies of *Id Quod Visum Placet* were packed and despatched and an engraving of the Good Shepherd, which had been the subject of the relief carving that Gill had done for Highbury Chapel in Bristol, was begun on 10 November. This was to be an ordination card for Desmond Chute and was printed with David Jones's aid on 25 November. Gill spent another day making prints for the Society of Wood Engravers Exhibition. To this Gill sent some of his old engravings and noted, in a letter to Joanna, that David Jones sent some "fine" work. Frank Rutter, however, reviewing in *The Sun-*

day Times, only mentions Jones somewhat carpingly because he included some copper engravings "which, strictly speaking, should not be in a wood engraving exhibition" (28.11.26).

Gill was heavily engaged upon *Troilus and Criseyde* but he nonetheless found time to write an article on 'Distributism and Production', a subject he discussed with David Jones and Denis Tegetmeier.

It was during this time, with her growing realization that it would be impossible to have children with David Jones whose financial position was precarious, that Petra was increasingly drawn towards Tegetmeier who was spending a lot of time at Capel and, as Cecil Gill suggested, "came along with very fervent advances" (CG/DK WAC). One visible remain of Tegetmeier's time at Capel is the enormous wall painting, executed in a light-hearted style, of the history of lettering through the ages. As a cartoonist, Tegetmeier was gently subversive though his work became more heavily didactic in the late 1930s.

Work continued on *Troilus and Criseyde* throughout December and Robert Gibbings visited Capel to discuss the project. In his book *Coming Down the Wye* Gibbings gave a picture of winter dinners at Capel that took place "by candlelight at the long refectory table, everyone wearing overcoats or shawls". René Hague, who came for Christmas, gave a picture of the phallocratic pattern of the nightly discussions:

> It was after dinner that most of the talking was done, the unfortunate
> girls still slaving at the sink, stove or spinning wheel...(RH DJ 25).

At Christmas, with Mary, Betty, Joanna and Gordian in France, Gill, Petra, David Jones and René Hague dined with the Attwaters on Christmas Day. Gill and Petra had both been "too much pressed with work" (EGDC 18.12.26 GLF) to accompany those journeying to join Joanna on 22 December. Fr. Joseph, who was suspected of having pleurisy, could only celebrate Mass on 25 and 26 December, and Gill wrote to Caldey to ask for somebody to look after him.

Despite the fact that in his *Autobiography* Gill writes very eloquently about Capel, looking back on it, as he looked back on Ditchling, as a kind of paradise, there were signs that he was finding it difficult. Writing to Desmond Chute earlier in the year, at the time of his first acquaintance with Salies and contemplating its ideal conditions of life he wrote, "I do not at present regard it as involving departure from C-y-ff" (LET 211). From that remark it is evident that the question of quitting was in the back of his mind. Gill was still searching for the ideal situation and, for all its blessings, Capel wasn't quite ideal. By the third week of the new year Gill ended his last long stay at Capel-y-ffin. Thereafter he was never in residence for longer than four weeks at a time and more often than not he stayed for a period of no more than a few days.

8. The Engravings of Eric Gill and David Jones

Eric Gill

The 1920s saw a revival of the art of wood engraving and Eric Gill, Gwen Raverat, Noel Rooke, Robert Gibbings and John Nash founded the Society of Wood Engravers in 1920. In some notes made in 1924, Gill listed the pros and cons of such a society: if there were the dangers of connoisseurship, high prices, snobbery and aestheticism, there were the benefits of discussion, the encouragement of certain standards, labour exchange and the sale of prints through exhibitions.

The brother of John Nash, Paul, who was elected to the society in 1921, was the engraver who consistently made the most varied experiments and who appeared to be the most aware of the severe and exciting work that had been done by the German Express-ionists and of the bold fluidity in the use of this medium by artists like Gauguin and Kandinsky. John Nash, for instance, used abstract forms in his engravings to express the events of Genesis such as *The Division of Light from the Darkness* in a way that Gill or Jones seem never to have considered. Yet nobody in the twenties appeared to go as far as Edward Wadsworth had done during his Vorticist period in utilizing the medium's capacity for the powerful assertion of bold forms, although Gibbings was capable of striking designs in which unanchored black shapes were stranded impressively on the white page. A little later, Gordon Craig made dramatic use of modernist abstraction in his engravings for *Hamlet* and about the same time Henry Moore brought an expressive vigour to the medium. There was, however, a consensus that the nature of the medium was essentially linear and it was Noel Rooke, one of the most conservative members of The

101

Society of Wood Engravers, who had returned to the Central School of Arts and Crafts where he had been a student at the same time as Gill, and taught between 1912 and 1924 a generation of young wood engravers. It can be noted that much subsequent English wood engraving is of a rather tame and conservative, neo-romantic nature.

In the same year that the Society of Wood Engravers had been set up, Harold Midgely Taylor had founded the Golden Cockerel Press as a co-operative. This proving impossible, Taylor rethought his original idea and re-oriented the press to the production of fine printing. Soon Taylor became ill and in 1924 the Press came under the direction of Robert Gibbings. As an engraver Gibbings was, by this time, beginning to turn in a more quietly illustrative direction, but he shared with Eric Gill the distinctive procedure of carving out large areas from a block to achieve a black line print. This was a lengthy and difficult job and both men entrusted this task to Ralph John Beedham. Beedham had been an apprentice engraver at the end of the nineteenth century and had learned lettering from Gill at Ditchling where his book, *Wood Engraving*, had been published by St. Dominic's Press in 1920. Without this *formschnieder* (the man who cuts or 'scorps' away the block in order to produce a black line print) neither Gill nor Gibbings could have achieved such a large output.

After the somewhat rough and ready printing at St. Dominic's Press, Ditchling, Gibbings gave Gill the opportunity to engrave for a high-quality press. Douglas Cleverdon suggests that the Golden Cockerel, which became a great press under Gibbings's guidance, was especially distinguished by the quality of its wood engraving rather than by its typography. *The Times*, however, in a review of an exhibition of engravings at the St. George's Gallery, wrote of "the harmonious relation" between typography and illustration in the productions of the Golden Cockerel Press (20.10.27). Certainly this was one of the aims of Robert Gibbings:

> The size and shape of the type determines the space left for decoration, and not until the type has been set and the page proofed does the artist begin his work (LM XXV 145).

Furthermore "the type is set by hand; only by so doing can the spacing be controlled, only by so doing can the page remain 'human' "(LM XXV 145). The quality of the press's work was further secured by the fact that they employed among the most accomplished and interesting engravers of the day including John and Paul Nash, David Jones and Eric Gill.

It was not only that Gill began to work for Robert Gibbings, "a printer and publisher who made definite demands" (EEG 1929), but also the fact of the remoteness of Capel that accounts for Gill's particular concentration on engraving during these years. At Capel Gill began to number his engravings and there is a prodigious total of two hundred and eighty blocks and plates made during this four year period. Gill worked quickly, perhaps too quickly. Criticism from Fr. Newman of the engravings for *Art and Love* perceptively informed Gill that "You're not giving yourself time to let ideas shape themselves as you would yourself *have* them shaped" (Let 13.2.27 WAC).

The Golden Cockerel commissions were the projects that most consistently concentrated Gill's energy during this period. *The Song of Songs* which he began thinking about in February 1925 occupied much of his time from July to October of that year. *Troilus and Criseyde* took the best part of a year from mid-1926 to mid-1927 and *The Canterbury Tales*, specimens of which were drawn in December 1927, engaged him from May 1928 for the next couple of years. Robert Gibbings recalls that "Eric was the perfect collaborator. He was always ready to accept a suggestion. Not only modest about his capabilities but modest also about the prices he asked for his work" (RG BC 2 2 102).

The first project that Gill undertook with the Golden Cockerel Press did not proceed along the ideal collaborative lines suggested above. Originally this work was to have been done in such a manner at Ditchling for reasons that Gill set out in a letter to the author of the book in question, his sister Enid Clay:

> I find that unless the printing and the typography and engraving are all done to match and under one control the result is a failure. You see, engravings are as much a part of *book making* as of *illustration*. They don't merely illustrate the text, they also decorate the book. Therefore the engraver and printer *must* be one 'firm' (1.3.24 WAC).

It is hardly surprising that with such views Gill proved to be the "ideal collaborator" for Gibbings. In fact, with the break away from Ditchling, what happened was that Clay sent the manuscript to Gibbings and Gill sent the engravings,and it was not possible to develop that "harmonious relation" for which the press was becoming famous (viz JD TR 9). Nonetheless *Sonnets and Verses* was, according to *The Observer* review, "printed with dignity and comeliness by the Golden Cockerel Press, and it has wood-engravings by Mr. Eric Gill one of our greatest masters in the medium" (31.5.25). Certainly, in some of Gill's engravings for the book there is a delicacy that eludes him in later work. The softness created by the gently hatched white lines subdues the starkness of his mannered forms and gives a pleasing and tentative texture for the eye to look at. But the correspondence between brother and sister reveals, at one point, Gill's willingness to be satisfied with the less than accomplished; concerning the engraving 'Death and the Lady' he wrote, "I'm v. sorry the faces and hands aren't better done — too difficult" (18.11.24 WAC).

During 1924 Gill produced a number of interesting individual woodcuts including *The Bee Sting* where the pain of a sting in the forearm twists a shaven female nude figure into an arched and revealing posture. Gill also printed this impressive design in intaglio with and without pubic hair. During the Capel years Gill came to favour the intaglio process which had first been used with woodblock as recently as 1916. The process demands the rubbing of ink into a cut line and then the plate is wiped clean. The resulting print gives the impression of the black line technique but involves much less effort. As Gill noted, it was a simpler process than copperplate and it gave "a more tender line" (WA 1 29). The only disadvantage with it is that the considerable pressure of printing crushes the softer wood of the block and only a limited number of prints can be pulled before the texture of the harder grain begins to assert itself, although that, as Gill noted, can be very pleasant (WA 1 29). Because Gill obtained a copper press and because, as he observed, "trade printers were unfamiliar" with intaglio, happily "the artist must do his own printing" (WA 1 29). Gill enjoyed experimenting with intaglio versions of designs that he had printed in the conventional manner. While certain of these are successful the method tends to reveal the shortcomings in the design and the novelty of the method, as the critic of *The Observer* noted, "may antagonize the pedant" (review of 1925 Redfern Gallery Exhibition).

More often than not Gill relied upon a stylized linearity, often to the detriment of individual characterization, but around 1924 he seemed to be unusually interested in character and psychology. The zinc engraving of Gordian in profile with its graceful play of hatched lines has an intriguing ambiguity about it. The Lowinsky portraits executed in the same month, October 1924, have a kind of Victorian exactitude in their representation of personality although in this case the greys are almost too fine resulting in a quasi-silhouette effect. The faces in *Safety First*, engraved for the *Labour Woman* between 28 and 30 October have a varied vitality that we do not normally associate with Gill's work. However, there is one face on the raft which appears unfinished. Is this void a design decision or an oversight, the result of Gill's habit of working quickly? The engraving shows the guardians of capitalist society against the horizon in a self-involved, arrogant and indifferent grouping while in the fore and mid-ground dynamic trades-unionists on a raft pull clamouring women from the waves. Perhaps the point would have been as well made without the explicit figures representing the pillars of the community. Their emblematic predictability in contrast to the foreground figures both compromises their alleged power and authority and considerably undermines the strength of the design; blocking them out reveals a supple and even powerful work.

For the Golden Cockerel Press edition of *The Song of Songs* with a text prepared by Fr. John O'Connor, Gill executed eighteen engravings in black line and the Press published thirty copies that were hand coloured only one of which was done by Gill himself. There is a slick, period feel about most of Gill's work on this project and the result is, at best, uneven. Among the often awkward, often saccharine woodcuts, Gill does make clever use of the folds of bedclothes. In *Ibi Docebo Me* these folds are somehow more expressive than the rather wooden figures and in other woodcuts Gill puts the decorative potential of swathing drapery to good and bold effect. Physical proximity is generally treated skilfully though sometimes, and this might be attributable to the influence of an Indian aesthetic, there appears to be a stilted or awkward quality about the figures. Fr. John O'Connor was particularly eager that Gill should "illustrate that passage when Solomon (who gets greasier and heavier as he goes on with the dancer) says: The junction of thy thighs falls like a necklet &c..." (WAC). While the woodcut of *The Dancer* before the king remains in the realm of costume drama one wonders if Gill's accuity in his treatment of the "greasy" King was not the result of a privileged personal insight into that voyeuristic condition. The writhing, restraining, crossed leg is the kind of expressive touch that we do not expect to find in Gill's work.

There was the inevitable clerical indignation at what was considered to be too explicit ("this sad country" where "sexual perversion is rife" — Fr. Austin WAC) although Desmond Chute noted that one of his Italian friends had commented that *The Song of Songs* was "not pornographic, because the archaism of the style sterilizes 'the matter' " (DC Let WAC). Sadly such "archaism" or "convention", as Chute interpreted the word, is a prophylactic against more than offence.

Gill was heading for another clash with the clergy by undertaking, in 1926, to engrave some illustrations for E. Powys Mathers's *Procreant Hymn* in which physical union between man and woman is taken as a symbol of the universal importance of creation. Gill produced two sets of copper engravings for the *Procreant Hymn*; one set was for publication with the poem and the other was for private subscription, the main difference between them being whether or not the erect penis was displayed. While the *Times Literary Supplement* reviewer of the publicly printed book noted that Gill strove "to purify and universalize" the "primarily sensuous" appeal "by an exquisite formality" (8.7.26) one order for the subscription set read, "Only send this if you are certain it will go through the American customs" (WAC); Ezra Pound who "never did think much of Mr. Gill or Henglish Hawt anyway" (EPL 228), when shown *The Song of Songs* had likewise wondered if that would get past those puritanical watchdogs of American morality.

In 1926 Gill engraved the *Passio Domini Nostri Jesu Christi* (Chapters 26 & 27 of Matthew's Gospel in Latin) and the project resulted in a typical mixture of good and bad that lacked stylistic homogeneity. There is a degree of inventiveness, an attempt to use aspects of an earlier visual language but this is not always invigorated by a contemporary vitality. The familiar effects of costume drama, saccharine expression and banality, to a large extent, vitiate these woodcuts.

It is the unsuccessful attempt at eclecticism or the transgression of moods that John Rothenstein reacted against in Gill's *Troilus and Criseyde*. Here, for example, as Rothenstein pointed out, a realistically portrayed modern woman reclines on a stylized plant in a somewhat uncomfortable mixture of ancient and modern. Also, in the *Troilus* Gill clothed some of the scenes such as 'The Meeting of Troilus and Criseyde' with a kind of ecclesiastical dignity and this is far from the spirit of Chaucer's poem where Christianity is added almost as an afterthought. Other, more appropriate engravings such as 'Approaching Dawn' utilize the sensual potential of flowing drapery of which Gill had made good use in *The Song of Songs*. In 'Approaching Dawn' there is an erotic movement created by the differing rhythms and patterns of the bedclothes though this is somewhat compromised by the sweet and stolid lovers. Otherwise, composite images like the dream of the dying warrior are fractured; Gill does not possess David Jones's skill in the integration or juxtaposition of diverse images. Overall, Gill seems to mistake the dignity and gravity of Chaucer and, at the same time, to miss his wit, though perhaps this is captured in some of the decorative borders. Writing later to R.A. Walker, Gill stated that

> the borders are simply decoration — their *raison d'être* is not illustration — the artist must efface himself. In the Troilus, in fact, there was *too much* variety in the borders — too many different sorts. The book was 'jumpy' (7.9.28 WAC).

The page with border reproduced here, however, in which a man shimmies up towards a woman who, in turn, points to higher things seems to reflect the Platonic dimension of the poem in an apt manner. Some borders might prove distracting, some might be excuses for Gill's "little naughtinesses" but the layout of *Troilus and Criseyde* with the lovely wide empty space at the bottom of each page was a great success. As with the *Passio* the relationship between word and image was largely pleasing. Gill's engravings nearly always look better in relation to typography just as they have more impact in their original hand-printed form than when they have been reproduced, particularly when there has been an enlargement.

Apart from the work for the major Golden Cockerel Press com-

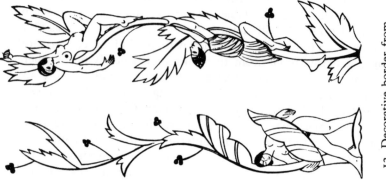

13. Decorative border from *Troilus and Criseyde*

12. 'Approaching Dawn' from *Troilus and Criseyde*

missions, during the Capel period Gill continued to produce some random engravings as well as the usually less than successful work that he engraved to illustrate some of his own pamphlets. Engraving is used, predictably, as an opportunity for erotic deliciation; a *Daily Mirror* photograph of two skaters in counter arabesque gave Gill the idea to engrave them in their revealing position, in the first state naked, and in the second state of the engraving, semi-nude. There is an engraving of an erect penis entitled 'The most precious ornament'. *The Woman Bending* of 1926 was made less of a study in form and more of an object of prurient delectation in the second state by the addition of a nipple. The work remains however less deliberately provocative than *The Chinese Maidservant* which Gill engraved in a similar pose in 1929 but with the figure tantalizingly undraped rather than naked. Count Kessler justifiably considered Gill's erotic work to be "rather cold" and when he showed some engravings to Aristide Maillol, the French artist found them *"pas mal, mais trop facile"* (SPE 68). One erotic work of a more darkly suggestive nature is *Eve* (1926) carved on sycamore which gave, in certain printings, a grainy texture to the print. A more purely formal interest in the female body was revealed in a small experiment in 1926 with a multiple tool (p.66), a graver with a number of small cutting edges that produced a series of fine white lines. It is a manner that Gill might profitably have pursued. *St. Bernadette*, despite her slightly cloying face, is a good example of an elegant, bold and simple design and the *Dame aux balles colorée s* is a fun piece of design, particularly when the *balles* are *colorées*. A portrait of Inigo Jones for the cover of *The Architect's Journal* showed that Gill was able to work in a style imitative of older wood engravings even if he was less successful in the more complicated matter of stylistic eclecticism.

As the decorative borders of *Troilus* had modern nudes disporting themselves in a quasi-medieval visual context, so the nudes peeping out from behind the foliage in the borders to *The Canterbury Tales* look like utterly modern flirts. It's not that some of Chaucer's tales aren't ribald, it's just that Gill cannot make a successful marriage between a medieval vision and his modern fantasy. Gill can rarely liaise, as David Jones can, between a medieval feeling or subject and a robust modernity of execution. Some of *The Canterbury Tales* border figures would be more appropriate on a programme for the *Folies Bergères* than on the pages of Chaucer's rich poem. Speaight felt that much of Gill's work on this project was mechanical and that this was the result of Gill having too much to do. Certainly we know that Gill worked quickly and did not take the same painstaking care that Jones took with each commission. In *The Canterbury Tales* there are felicities such as the way in which the borders burgeon into illustrations to mark the breaks between tales and there is a 'sameness' in the rest of the borders which is, as Gill wrote to R.A. Walker, "just precisely what I have aimed at" (7.9.28 WAC). Unfortunately, one by-product of this 'sameness' is a tendency to slickness or facility. *The Canterbury Tales* was a large undertaking and it appeared in annual instalments commencing in 1929. As Gill went on into the thirties his engraving often became absurdly fussy as if he was merely demonstrating technical mastery of a medium. The engravings and capitals for *The Four Gospels* are intelligently and excitingly placed in relation to the typography on the page but in themselves the images are cluttered or crude or mannered or ill-thought or needlessly and irritatingly fancy. Indeed much of Gill's engraved work in the thirties is irrational and ugly and is often marked by a very 'period' feel. During the Capel years however, while Gill sacrificed some of the more primitive vitality and occasional roughness to which he had been disposed at Ditchling, he achieved, in his collaborations with the Golden Cockerel Press, a high degree of professionalism. As Desmond Chute observed, the books were "beautifully printed" and the blocks fitted "in with the type, as they never did under Hilary" (Let WAC).

David Jones

In England during the eighteenth century Thomas Bewick developed the expressive capacity of wood-engraving by reversing the dominant black line method into that of the white line technique which was capable of subtly suggesting both texture and the play of light upon a subject. And since the early eighteenth century illustrators have used the very durable boxwood which was transported from Turkey and south-eastern Asia, thoroughly seasoned and then cut crossways so that the polished end-grain could be used to produce fine details uncomplicated by the larger cross grain of the wood. This gives rise to a print in which blacks, whites and greys harmonize in a delicately balanced whole and it is within this tradition that the bulk of modern English wood engravers have worked. David Jones aspired to this kind of harmony in works like *The Book of Jonah* and *The Chester Play of the Deluge*.

In no other medium was Jones so much influenced by Eric Gill. Even though it was Desmond Chute who actually began to teach Jones to engrave at Ditchling, Cleverdon suggests that this can only have lasted a matter of weeks (DC EEG 3). Jones's tutelage continued under Eric Gill and, as the artist notes, he "gradually became able to engrave tolerably enough to do small jobs for Mr. Hilary Pepler's private Press". Jones goes on to note that his work "at this time was stylized, conventionalized, and heavily influenced by theory, and imitative of primitive Christian art. Nevertheless the discipline of engraving — of doing jobs however badly, the sharpening of tools, and the atmosphere of workshop rather than studio, and the clarifying ideas of Mr Gill were...of very great value" (DJL). Jones's work at Ditchling, despite such humility, was often experimental and increasingly accomplished. Although wood-engraving for St Dominic's Press was not considered self-consciously as an 'art form' Jones was developing into a skilled artist in that medium. Yet, as with Gill, it was the commissions for quality presses which were to establish Jones's reputation as an engraver.

Robert Gibbings of the Golden Cockerel Press commissioned Jones to execute thirty-seven illustrations and five maps for a two volume Quarto edition of *Gulliver's Travels*. Jones maintained that the Press called in art students to hand-colour the book and he subsequently removed the colour from his own copy (LC 9), but Douglas Cleverdon suggests that Jones must have "agreed to the colouring":

> there exist a couple of coloured artist's proofs on india-paper, which must have been coloured by David himself; and the prospectus (of which a coloured proof was found among his papers) definitely states that many of the blocks will be hand-coloured under his care (DC DJE 11)

Jones didn't particularly enjoy the project in any case as it hung over him during his first trip to Caldey when he longed to be painting. Furthermore there "were too many wood engravings to do" and it was "such a boring book! Utopias, positive or negative, are all boring" (LC 72). Yet in the engravings that Jones produced for this work there is an organizational deftness which, despite their smallness, gives both a sense of size and makes the viewer conscious of size, an important and mutable element in *Gulliver's Travels*. Forms are squeezed into the small squares and rectangles with ingenuity and power. As usual, Jones demonstrates a knowledge of contemporary art movements; *Interchang - ing the Occiputs* is almost as vicious as a work by a contemporary German *Neue Sachlichkeit* artist. Likewise, the thick black lines in the top left and bottom right of *Female Yahoo Embraces Gulliver* are reminiscent of Gauguin's woodcuts and this engraving, with its mask-like head, has a primitive expressionist quality — particularly so in the hand coloured version where it appears red, green and flesh coloured. The breasts crushed against the buttocks, the Yahoo's arm round Gulliver's genitals, and the shading which takes on the sexual connotation of pubic hair makes this image as erotic as anything that Gill produced. By comparison, an experimental engraving that Gill made of a female Yahoo in 1926 is an unexpressive figure that lacks the sexual charge of Jones's earlier woodcut. Likewise *Whore on the Back Stairs*, with her ambiguous pickpocketing action and bulging rotundities is similarly sexually charged. There is a warmth in Jones's handling of the medium, an innate sensuality that, for all his sexuality, escapes Gill.

If Jones was annoyed that work on Gulliver prevented him from doing more watercolours during his first trip to Caldey, the experience of being on the island helped with certain engravings; *Ship and Long Boat in Bay* shows a Caldey bay and in it Jones resolved the difficult problem of representing the sea by patterning it in a series of curved cones. There is, in all the engravings for *Gulliver*, evidence of Jones's patience in preparation of each design, his willingness to consider each as a unique artistic problem to be resolved rather than as the next illustration in a job of work. Jones's first instructor in the medium, Desmond Chute, in a letter to Gill, noted that *Gulliver* was good and praised particularly the "technical achievement" (22.2.26 WAC).

Inspired by his first visit to Caldey, Jones made a woodcut of *Tenby from Caldey* when he was at Capel in July 1925. The view is familiar to us from several watercolours and Jones's usual sensitivity to the hill rhythms of the landscape is also achieved in this medium. In the foreground, the fish-like hillocks not only sort well with the sea beyond but give a fluid, shimmering feeling to the work. Jones articulates no less than eight cows, giving them a bulk which they often lack in their sketchy *faux-naif* treatment in his watercolours done at Capel and Pigotts.

If this engraving suggests the diminishing of Gill's influence, Jones considered *The Book of Jonah* which was published in 1926 by the Golden Cockerel Press to be "pure Eric" though nonetheless good (LC 10). While the influence is visible in the use of the nimbus and the aureole, devices that considerably weaken the designs, there is a formal energy and sophisticated use of texture that is not often present in Gill's work. There is control and variety of line in the woodcut of the spouting whale and cohesion in the texturing in the woodcut of the whale disgorging 'Jonah upon the Dry Land' (the whale's chops and the sides of the cliff). If the initial engraving of the 'Word of the Lord coming to Jonah' does appear to be Gillian, notice how Jones arrestingly splits the engraving into white line and black line technique and gives us a vision of Nineveh as a Futurist metropolis. How skilfully Jones conveys the sense of underwater space in 'The waters compassed me about'. How intelligently disposed are the L-shaped arrangements on facing pages of the people of Nineveh praying and of the expressive figure of Jonah in his booth on his island outside the city.

Jones's ability to articulate forms into tight, inventive and audacious compositions is nowhere so apparent as in the ten engravings he did for *The Chester Play of the Deluge* which engaged him from 1926 until the autumn of 1927. This is a quality in his work that re-emerges with the most successful of the late mythological paintings that he made from 1940 onwards. In *The Chester Play of the Deluge* the figure forms do owe something to Gillian mock-medievalism although the poses are always more originally and more expressively contrived than Gill's own. There is energy, wit and, as always, a quiet utilization of continental developments in art. In *The Chester Play of the Deluge* Jones demonstrates the medium's subtlety; as Albert Garret notes:

14. *The Chester Play of the Deluge*

114

> While Jones's wood engravings are very solid in the black, his greys
> are very evenly distributed. In some of his wood engravings, his greys
> skim through the composition as lightly as wind swept cirrus
> clouds...some lines little more than a scratch...(HWE 277).

Jones's habit of wanting to fit everything in is becoming evident
though here it is often achieved felicitously; there is much invention in the labyrinthine organization of details and several engravings are masterly. The powerful 'Great Rain', and the witty
and affectionate 'Beasts after their kind' (V) and 'The entry into
the Ark' (VI), which was Jones's own favourite, are all examples
of Jones's command of the medium. The fifth and sixth engravings are displayed on the facing pages eight and nine of the book.
In these the individual characteristics of the walking animals syn-
copate the purposeful walking rhythm that the artist sets up. For
example, on the left hand page, the leopards are seen in determined profile whereas the bears are wittily twisted towards the
spectator. On the right hand page the whole march culminates in
the exclamation-mark-like effect of the leopards entering the ark;
they turn their heads to confront the spectator saying, as it were,
'We've done it!'. After considering work by Gill these engravings
appear so subtle, so expressive, so thought. But unfortunately,
Jones's high hopes for the project were dashed in the printing. As
Cleverdon records:

> In order to meet the publishing deadline, the preliminary dampening
> of the sheets was omitted, and the engraved blocks were printed
> (simultaneously with the text) on a hard unsympathetic hand-made
> Batchelor paper.

This Batchelor Paper is a pure rag paper and because of its hardness it is essential that it be dampened before use. Cleverdon
continues:

> Having devoted himself to the engravings with such intense concen-
> tration, David was deeply disappointed with the book. In fairness to
> the Golden Cockerel Press, it must be said that David, a perfectionist
> himself, was never satisfied with anything less than perfection in
> those who worked with him; nor would he compromise in any way
> to make their task less difficult.' (DC DJE 13).

The Artist which Jones engraved for Gill's pamphlet *Chris-*
tianity and Art again reveals his skill in fluid and graceful articu-

lation. Here the animals curve sinuously around the artist at work and the bird's beak wittily counterpoints the artist's brush. Above the roof of the artist's studio the work becomes less effective — even the deer is the least inventive of the animals; blocking out this weak area considerably strengthens the rest and allows the leopard's spots at the bottom to echo more obviously the spots on the studio roof making the design tighter. The sensuous and absorbed artist inhabits an ambiguous space which is created by Jones's use of cubist devices such as the absence of centralized perspective. Thus Jones expresses the strange fluidity that the practise of art creates: the interplay of matter and spirit.

Not all of Jones's engravings of this period are noteworthy. *The Great British Public* is a rather heavy-handed piece of symbolism in which a dandyish donkey in plus-fours is caught in the web of American finance; it was an illustration for E. C. Bentley's 'Ballade of Plain Common Sense' and could have been better left to Eric Gill. A commissioned Christmas card, *Coach and Horse in Winter Landscape* (1926) is a slight, trivial, jobbish piece of work and has nothing in common with the Christmas cards that Jones engraved for his friends each year between 1921 and 1929 which were often works of considerable beauty. We should remember however that during the Ditchling and Capel period Jones earned his meagre living by engraving and by the occasional sale, particularly from 1927 onwards, of watercolours. The £4 that Desmond Chute paid for his book-plate *The Fishers of Men*, designed in 1925, must have been most welcome to the artist.

The beginnings of Jones's experiments in copper engraving reflected, as Cleverdon notes, "the fluid...style" (DC DJE 11) that Jones had developed in his Welsh watercolours of this period. This is even visible to some extent in the small *Nant Honddu* which Cleverdon suggests may well be Jones's first attempt in the medium (DC DJE 11). It is an enchanting landscape that presents a quiet spirituality untrammelled by religious iconography. There is an eerie, fairytale feeling about the engraving which, apart from a small house, is devoid of animal or human presence. A daring large empty space in the middle of the small work adds to the sense of charged stillness.

During 1926 Jones went on to produce a limited edition of twenty of each of four copper engravings (*Ponies on a Welsh Hill Slope, Reclining Cat, Puma* and *The Crucifixion*). These so im-

THE ENGRAVINGS OF ERIC GILL AND DAVID JONES

pressed Douglas Cleverdon
> that as a young bookseller, greatly daring, I asked David to engrave
> on copper eight illustrations with headpiece and tailpiece, for Cole-
> ridge's *Rime of the Ancient Mariner* (DC DJE 12).

However, before undertaking this project, Jones, in London in the summer of 1927, engraved seven plates for Walter Shewring's translation of the *Seven Fables of Aesop* which was to be published in a limited edition by the Lanston Monotype Corporation. The most distinguished of these seven copper engravings is the beautifully composed *Lion and the Farmer*. The animal recaptures something of the quality of Jones's remarkable childhood animal drawings and the woman is languidly sensual (and is even more so in a surviving preliminary sketch).

Grace of line is something that Jones sought and achieved; he wrote years later in his *Introduction to the Rime of the Ancient Mariner* :

> I am of the opinion that the most specific beauty, that which belongs
> to copper-engraving, *sui generis*, is a lyricism inherent in the clean,
> furrowed free, fluent engraved line, as quintessentially linear as the
> painted lines on one type of Greek vase, or in Botticelli's...illustra-
> tions to the *Divina Commedia* or the purely linear designs in Anglo-
> Saxon illustrated MSS (DYG 188).

Jones tentatively suggested that his illustrations for *The Rime* might be engraved in wood, believing himself to be "better at wood" (DC DJE 14) but it was copper-engraving that Cleverdon particularly had in mind. The fact that he was a relative novice in that medium "precluded", thought Jones, "cleverness and any attempt at complexity" (DYG 188). Furthermore he found in the poem, "a deceptive surface ease and facility and a simplicity of artistry" (DYG 189) which he hoped to reflect in the style that he adopted for the series. Jones

> decided that simple incised lines reinforced here and there and as
> sparingly as possible by cross-hatched areas (e.g. the hull, masts,
> yards and spars of the stricken ship in the third full-page illustration),
> was the only way open to me. I decided also that these essentially
> linear designs should have an undertone over the whole area of the
> plate, partly as an aid to unification. This is easily and naturally
> achieved in copper-plate printing by not wiping the plate totally clean
> of ink before putting it in the press. (DYG 187)

Without this undertone, Jones added, the designs 'fall to pieces'.

Jones worked on the 150 to 200 preliminary drawings through-out the second half of 1928 and 1929 and while *The Rime of the Ancient Mariner* was not published until 1929 and hence outside the limitations of this book, it would seem suitable to make a few brief comments, particularly as increasing trouble with his eye-sight meant that this was to be Jones's last large project as an engraver.

Jones subjected Coleridge's poem to an idiosyncratic and speci-fically religious interpretation: in the second engraving the shot albatross appears 'crucified' against the mast and spar of the ship; in the fifth engraving the dead albatross appears hanging from the priestly neck of the mariner (Jones was to describe a rifle hanging from the neck of a wounded soldier in *In Parenthesis* as being "like the Mariner's white oblation" — IP 184).

The third engraving with large "slimy things" that crawled "with legs/ Upon the slimy sea", the flaming sun and the arbitrary lines of hatching that run like stress lines through the scene, builds up a disturbing atmosphere. Less successful is the fourth engraving of *Death and Life in Death*.. Here the skeleton has none of that macabre quality that we find in say Michael Wolgemut's *Dance of the Dead* from the *Nuremburg Chronicle* of 1493. An artist who was constantly looking backwards for his inspiration might well have drawn on such a source. And yet there is a feeling that the figures themselves are being shaken-up by fortune, no more self-determining than the dice they throw in their game of chance. Overall, the middle engravings, with their tilting horizons, decks and the consequent absence of verticals give an energy and move-ment to the series which is a quality that Jones always sought. Sadly, the first and last engravings have a more insipid, illustra-tional quality than the rest.

For David Jones *The Rime* provoked yet another manner of making a work of art; what lifts Jones's work above that of Gill's is not only the painstaking care that he takes with each project but also his constant searching, his artistic preoccupation with the right manner or mode in which to treat a particular subject. And not only was Jones more experimental, he was also more sensitive and curiously, often more sensual. While Jones was cap-able of errors of judgement, an occasional taste for the saccharine or, at times, a tendency towards a mannered medievalism, his is an achievement that is compromised by no fundamental dilemma such as that which dogged Gill's work. Apart from Gill's swiftness in discharging a commission which prohibited the application of that artistic intelligence which he so strongly advocated, there was that protective slickness which time and time again undermined his powers of expression. Jones, on the other hand, was always prepared to take the time to understand the particular problems of an artistic task. *The Times* reviewer of an exhibition of engravings at the St George's Gallery in October 1927, when contemplating the work of artists like Jones, Gill, Gibbings and Laboureur, found Jones's work to be 'the most imaginative" (20.10.27).

9. 1927 'To find a human life'

There was a good deal of reorganization in the early days of 1927 before Gill set off for Salies-de-Béarn. The Gills' bedroom was moved into the west wing of the monastery and Petra's weaving room was relocated. Amidst this upheaval Gill continued to work on the borders for *Troilus and Criseyde* and corrected proofs for *Art and Love* which Douglas Cleverdon was publishing under his own imprint in Bristol, a situation not altogether welcomed by the Golden Cockerel Press who were nonetheless printing the work.

For David Jones 1927 began unhappily. Petra Gill had come to realize that her fiancé was a great procrastinator who, in reality, would never take the decisive step to marriage. She broke off their engagement when she decided to marry Denis Tegetmeier who had no qualms about trying to combine the practice of his arts with the responsibilities of family life; Jones had, on the other hand, since his early teens, considered it probable that his vocation would not accommodate marriage. While Petra's decision in some sense relieved him from what Hague calls "the burden of responsibility", it was also an enormous shock that helped to confirm in him a pessimistic vision which he nonetheless confronted bravely (DG 42). Despite the fact that Jones spent a lot of time in bed at Capel it is perhaps significant that during this period of stress the doctor called to see him on 11 January.

Gill, en route to Salies-de-Béarn at the end of the month, stopped in London and spent one night talking to Denis Tegetmeier. Gill was, as we have seen, enormously fond of Jones but after the breaking of the engagement he realized that the proposed marriage, because of Jones's tendency to indecision, could never have taken place. Writing to Desmond Chute three weeks later, Gill suggested that not only had things worked out for the best but that the worst of the crisis had passed quickly:

> Poor old D.J. was v. cut up at first but he's all right now & really much happier I think. The idea of marriage 'put the wind up' him horribly — it was an impending doom — & fond as he was of Petra it was not 'married love'. As for Petra she's a different person & so is Denis T. DJ is at present at Caldey — not the best place for him according to my way of thinking — but he's fond of the place & is painting the rocks and the sea....Fr. John O'C was all for Petra's breaking it off years ago. He said David would never marry. I think he's right. (11.3.27 GLE).

At first, Gill only stayed in Salies for two weeks with his wife and Betty, Joanna and Gordian. He worked on *Troilus* and wrote a lecture on 'Architecture and Sculpture' which he returned to England to deliver on 16 February at the University of Manchester. Gill made this lecture, which was eventually published by the Royal Manchester Institution, the opportunity to make 'a statement' on the relationship between the architect and the sculptor and on the role of the sculptor in relation to contemporary styles of building. Sculptors, Gill suggested, had little or no part to play in modern building where the best architecture to be found was "without any embellishment" (A&S 29). He brought the lecture to a close with a familiar but vitally important conclusion:

> I am only saying that a civilization depending upon the reduction of the great majority of workers to a position of irresponsibility is in the nature of things an unstable civilization, because contrary to the nature of man (A&S 29).

The Manchester Guardian, which published a précis, found the talk "penetrating" (17.2.27). Fr. Austin was "entirely grateful for the lecture" and W.R. Lethaby, the leader of the Arts and Crafts Movement, to whom Gill had sent a copy, noted in a letter that he was in "entire agreement" with the impassioned last part (WAC).

After nine days in England visiting London, Manchester, Waltham St Lawrence and Bristol, but significantly not visiting Capel, Gill returned to Salies and stayed there until the end of April.

15. Salies de Béarn with St Vincent's Church

Completely different in character and climate from the wilderness of Capel-y-ffin, the older part of Salies-de-Béarn is an idyllic town of stone houses that dates from the seventeenth and eighteenth centuries. These are crowded in small streets and alley ways that lead off the *Place du Bayàa* and *Place de la Trompe*. Houses overhang the lazy river, their balconies decked with flowers and around and about the town are the rolling hills that, to the south, become the foothills of the Pyrenees. The *Villa des Palmiers* which Elizabeth Bill bought and which the Gills furnished was to be found a little out of the old town, up the steep *Rue du Château*. Close to the bottom of this street stood St Vincent's where the family attended Mass. Gill wrote in his *Autobiography* that

> At last, at last we had the chance to live for a time in a human city which was in some sort a holy city, and to live a life, a city life which was a holy life. (233).

While Count Kessler had noted that, faced with the choice between London and Capel, Gill had decided to "try the wilderness first", Gill was now thinking that he had found the kind of "civilized town life" which in England had "long since been submerged in the universal vulgarity of our commercialism" (AUT 230). He wrote that he didn't particularly want "to go to the south of France to find a human life" but that he wanted "to find a human life" (AUT 230). Mary Gill, in a letter to Fr. Rope, noted the dilemma that began to provoke questions about the plausibility of staying in Wales: "...Capel...is a most glorious place. We never want to leave it — but it is a very strenuous life." Whereas, with reference to Salies, she wrote that "it is good for the young ones especially, to live under quite normal Catholic conditions — which is quite impossible in Protestant England..." (10.3.27 WAC).

Mary Gill described to Fr. Rope the benefits of their new life:

> Eric is very busy — we are enjoying the quiet and peace of this little Catholic town....This is our first experience of a Catholic parish — and we find it both restful and invigorating and at the same time spiritually refreshing for it is a very much alive parish (10.3.27 WAC).

In a letter written on the following day, Gill vouched that

> The daily round is all that I could wish......The villa is about 15 minutes walk from the centre of town and as I've got a workroom down in town it's a nice little walking excercise for me. Mass at 8.0. Breakfast at the Café in the 'Place' (at which one or other of the girls join me), work till 12.30, Déjeuner 12.45. Work from 2.0 to 6.0. Evening Prayers at the Church & Benn. 6.15. Then home to supper — reading & music till bed time 10.0.& that's that, & one day follows another. I call it an earthly paradise (LET 216- 17).

What is interesting is that at Salies Gill carried out much the same work as he did at Capel but under much less arduous winter conditions. While the climate, the density of the population and the mode of life were vastly different from Capel-y-ffin, Gill saw life at Salies as "perfectly in harmony with our life at Capel" (AUT 229-30). Furthermore, while Gill was enjoying the mild winter in the south of France, Laurie Cribb, his "noble pupil" (AUT 219) and assistant was back at Capel cutting out the background for the Rossall School Memorial which Gill would carve later in the year. Gill himself continued to work on *Troilus and Criseyde* for it was a big job — about sixty borders, five full page pictures and some initials.

At the end of February the family went to the Carnival, Gordian started school on 2 March and they read Dickens's *Bleak House* in the evenings and after that Conrad's *The Secret Agent* and Hardy's *The Woodlanders*. While they were deprived of Mary Gill's clavichord, Joanna had brought her harp, much to the annoyance of the other passengers on the train coming south from Paris. They visited nearby Bayonne to see the cathedral and the Musée Basque and the Musée Bonnat. They attended a concert in the parish hall and took many walks, their favourite being to nearby Sauveterre "with its terrace café a hundred feet above the rushing Gave" (AUT 234). On Palm Sunday the church was full of children with palm branches and Gill was impressed by the Passion sung by unaccompanied voices. He recorded in a letter to Desmond Chute that Salies "seems to do us good altogether.... Mary's getting as fat as anything, & B. P. & J. are all flourishing." (LET 217). Nonetheless, on 25 April, the Gill's minus Gordian, who stayed behind at school, left Salies to spend the summer back in Wales. En route Gill was delayed an extra day in Paris as he lost his purse. Paris appears to have made the usually careful Gill quite forgetful but the delay did give him an extra afternoon's drawing at the Chaumière.

Gill returned to London to a newly opened joint exhibition at the St George's Gallery of his own drawings and David Jones's watercolours. This exhibition was the result of the introduction by Eric Gill and H.S. Ede of David Jones to Arthur Howell, the owner of the gallery, in 1925. Howell on that occasion included a couple of Jones's pictures in an exhibition of the Modern English Watercolour Society. But when Jones returned several months later, Howell wrote:

> After he left I opened the portfolio and took out what was in it. The work seemed to me exquisite. Quite apart from the colour, and the design into which it was woven, there was here a charm, an imponderable delicacy and gentleness of vision, maturely handled, that was entirely personal.' (FVY 5-10)

Gill showed thirty-four figure studies "by arrangement with the Goupil Gallery" and David Jones showed twenty-seven watercolours, largely made at Capel-y-ffin or on Caldey. Some of Jones's titles were rather grand such as 'The Dolorous Mountain', 'Castle and a Thousand Hills', 'The High Mountains of Israel' but others were given the same simple titles by which they are known today: 'The Suburban Order' or 'The Dog on the Sofa'. Most of Gill's rather simple sketches were priced at three or four guineas and Jones's watercolours at between eight and twenty guineas. The show drew many spectators and was favourably reviewed in *G.K.'s Weekly*:

> This is the first show of Mr. David Jones, though as a wood engraver he must be well known...to those who care for the best modern woodcuts. In his water colours, an individual vision is combined with a formal quality of expression...breadth and simplicity of treatment...strong sense of design and charm of colour..(7.5.27).

For this debut Jones made an impressive showing. He demonstrated a firm control and wit in his articulation of cubist devices in a Brockley interior like *The Dog on the Sofa* and he showed his sensitivity to the emotional implications of atmospheric nuances of light and locality in the Welsh paintings. Add to these qualities Jones's acknowledged and growing mastery in the medium of wood engraving and it was clear that a major talent was in the process of coming rapidly to maturity.

In London for five days at the end of April and beginning of May, Gill drew the figure at Oliver Lodge's studio and saw much of David Jones. He also met René Hague, who according to Laurie Cribb who had seen him a month before, was

> very cheerful & comfortable — in fact extremely so! He was telling us that he now does a bit of Tub thumping in Hyde Park of all places — I should love to hear him — probably does it jolly well. He would have a gift for that sort of thing. (Let EG 20.3.27 WAC).

From 4 May Gill was at Capel working largely on *Troilus and Criseyde* for which he had already completed thirty-eight engravings in Salies during March and April. Towards the end of the month he was also working on designs for pictures for his pamphlet, *Art and Love*. Apropos of the St George's Gallery Exhibition which had closed on 11 May Gill wrote to Desmond Chute that it had been "quite successful, expecially from the point of view of David who sold nine paintings." Perhaps recalling the recent crisis with Petra, Gill went on to observe that Jones was 'well, but considerably sadder and wiser" (29.5.27 GLE).

On 28 May Douglas Cleverdon came for the weekend to discuss

the possibility of an edition of selected engravings. Gill was enthusiastic about the project although he had been disappointed by John Rothenstein's book which had just been published by Ernest Benn:

> I have no right to complain of the illustrations, though I regret the inclusion of some.... But the introduction is very disappointing.... Many of the facts are wrong and the style seems to be horribly impudent and patronizing (Let RAW 6.4.27 WAC).

Rothenstein's introduction, however, does not appear to be particularly unjust.

In his description of Capel Gill notes that the "eldest daughter managed the animals and the farm", Mary "did the baking and the two younger" girls "did the house and cooking" (AUT 228). But this pattern was about to be broken. On 1 June Gill's eldest daughter, Betty was twenty-two and her wedding to David Pepler was set for two days later. That same day Laurie Cribb was to be married and the services were held, one after the other, at the Catholic Church in Talgarth. After the Cribb's marriage at 8:30 a.m. Elizabeth Gill became Mrs Pepler. The rift between the groom's father and Eric Gill somewhat soured the occasion for Gill although he had agreed to the marriage with grudging accord. After exchanging "polite nothings", Gill and Hilary Pepler kept away from one another at the "awful party". As Gill had written to Desmond Chute:

> we are not 'satisfied' about B's marriage but could not prevent it. We believe David P. is a good, steady, honest & hard working young man & devoted to B. as she is to him (29.5.27 GLE).

On 22 June Gill went to Waltham St Lawrence to engrave initials for *Troilus and Criseyde*. In March, Moira Gibbings had given birth to twin boys and Robert Gibbings, whom Eric Gill described as "the dearest creature ever known" (Let DC 5.5.26 GLE), was, with four young mouths to feed, beginning to feel the pinch. But despite the pressing situation, Gibbings had no intention of altering the way in which the Golden Cockerel Press was run, and there was therefore discussion about even more ambitious projects for the future.

At Waltham the sexual experimentation continued; on 22 June, after drawing in the nude, it seems that Gill had his first experience of fellating somebody. He records in his diary an event that confirms his philophallicism:

> a man's penis & balls are very beautiful things.... The shape of the head of a man's erect penis is very excellent in the mouth. There's no doubt about this. I have often wondered — now I know.' (D 22.6.27).

Certainly, in his countless drawings of male genitalia, Gill shows a fascination with their shape. He is interested in geometric patterns deriving from penis and testicles and distorts the shapes into organic, almost Boschian curves. He formalizes them, he observes the penis in various states of erection and he paints it in lurid colours. Large tracts of his abandoned erotic novel constitute almost a hymn to the penis which, in one passage, develops into a celebration of a kind of auto-coitus:

> ...it grew stiffer — standing more out from his belly — now it was really stiff — it swung now pivotting...it arched slightly upwards — the foreskin retracting a little showing its pink peeping mouth...he exposed the whole head glistening red. Ah — How big!

After ejaculation, "the foreskin, no longer stretched as by a fruit too big for the basket, gently closes over his pearly peach" and the man's semen runs "between the folds of his arse, so that his arsehole like a rosy mouth receives a modicum of the gift intended for a woman's body" (WAC).

On the evening of 23 June, Gill was in Oxford with David Jones hearing G.K. Chesterton lecture at the French Club and on the following day in London they went to the Matisse exhibition and met René Hague and Donald Attwater in the evening. On 25 June Gill and Jones visited E. Powys Mathers, the author of the *Procreant Hymn*, at his flat in Lincoln's Inn Fields which was decorated with pornographic postcards. Gill confided to Jones that "If I were not a Catholic, I should have been like this" (SPE 179)! Yet didn't Gill share a similar enthusiasm for such things? On the back of an envelope posted in 1927, Gill drew, with great attention to detail, a penis penetrating the vagina, recording that it was drawn "from a photograph". On another occasion he complained that some German naturist magazines were a swindle because they didn't contain un-retouched photographs of completely naked people.

On 26 June the newly wedded Elizabeth and David Pepler joined Gill for lunch and afterwards they all went to tea at Oliver Lodge's studio. That evening David Jones and Denis Tegetmeier met each other for the first time since Tegetmeier's engagement to Jones's ex-fiancée, Petra. They talked and went out to supper with Gill, Attwater and the Peplers and Gill records that it was a "very nice meeting" (D 26.6.27).

David Jones had spent a good deal of the time engraving since the breaking of his engagement. He had done a frontispiece for the Gregynog Press edition of *Llyer y Pregethwr* (*The Book of Ecclesiastes*) in a style that was more densely packed than that which he had used in *The Book of Jonah*. During this period Jones had also been working on *The Chester Play of the Deluge* for the Golden Cockerel Press and he was justifiably pleased with what he achieved; writing to Douglas Cleverdon towards the end of June he called it his "sumptuous work", going on to say that "I believe it will really look good — if I may be allowed to say so!" (DC EDJ 14).

Gill spent 27 and 28 June at the solicitors preoccupied with the seemingly endless Ditchling wrangle, though one of the evenings passed agreeably at the Princess Theatre in Shaftesbury Avenue where Stravinsky himself was conducting three of his own ballets (D. 27.6.27).

Home again at the end of the month, Gill finished the initial for the last verse of *Troilus and Criseyde* on 1 July, eleven months after he had begun the project. The rest of that month passed quietly at Capel, Gill absorbed with sundry tasks. Quite a number of drawings of genitals were done and Gill drew an erotic sketch of 'Lady X de X' spreadeagled over a tapering bed wearing only stockings. This was drawn on the back of a wrapper for Churchman's Light Counter Shag — a humorous juxtaposition of words when one considers the opposing tensions in Gill's life.

At the end of the month and at the beginning of August Gill was off on a lightning trip to Salies to collect Gordian from school. On the return journey they spent a day in Paris where Gill "left G. sailing a boat" in the Jardin du Luxembourg while he drew at the *Academie Chaumière*.

August passed quietly at Capel. Gill was reading Proust's *Swann's Way* and Rousseau's *Confession*s. Fr. Gray came to visit as did Douglas Cleverdon who brought with him the photographer Methven Brownlee who shared Cleverdon's flat above the Bristol bookshop and "to whom Gill, Morison, Beatrice Warde and David Jones in turn became greatly attached"(SM&EG BC).

For David Jones August was very busy. Not only was he doing a wood engraving (*The Artist*) for Gill's *Christianity and Art* which was to be published by Donald Attwater under the pseudonym of Francis Walterson but he was also doing specimens for *Aesop's Fables* which Stanley Morison was to publish. For one week during the month Jones went to stay with Cleverdon in Bristol who recalls that he

> was a very agreeable companion, relishing the humorous, but with an inexorable urge to get a thing *right* whether it was a phrase, or a principle, or a brush stroke in a water-colour. All of us were devoted to him (DC DJE 15-16).

Every day that he was staying with Cleverdon Jones did a watercolour, usually looking towards the cathedral, from the studio above Cleverdon's shop.

Having already lost the helping hand of one daughter, the establishment at Capel suffered further diminishment early in September when Gill himself all but moved to London to centre his life on a studio in Glebe Place, Chelsea lent to him by his friend and patron Lord Howard de Walden. The location of this studio was convenient for David Jones as it was near St. Leonard's Terrace where, in the house of Tom Burns the young Catholic publisher, Jones met friends such as René Hague, Harman Grisewood and Burns himself who were, after Gill, the most important personal influences upon him in the succeeding decades. Burns was the motivating energy behind the short-lived magazine *Order* for which Jones provided a cover engraving (*The Unicorn*) and for which Gill wrote two articles: 'Repository Art' and '2d. Plain, 1d. Coloured'.

On 23 September Mary Gill arrived in London with Gordian and Gill took him on as far as Paris on his return journey to school. They stayed at the Hotel de l'Europe and did some sightseeing, and Gill saw his adopted son off from the Gare D'Orsay.

At the beginning of October, after being rather unwell in September, Jones found himself marooned in Tenby waiting for the seas to calm so that he could cross to Caldey Island. He wrote to

H.S. Ede that "It's very depressing — anyway being alone in a hotel always really drives me mad!" (DG 42), a particularly sad remark in light of the many lonely years Jones spent in a residential hotel towards the end of his life.

While Jones was painting on Caldey Island, hoping "to get some landscapes done before the summer ends" (DC DJE 16), Gill spent most of October in London carving and drawing and socializing with the usual set of friends. With only three days back in Capel, November passed very much in the same manner as October had done except that David Jones was back from Caldey. There were important exhibitions for both men during these months. Jones, as I have quoted, was singled out for particular praise at the St George's Gallery exhibition of engravings. At the Goupil Salon, amid some 253 works by artists as diverse as Renoir, Vlaminck, Derain, Meninsky, John Nash and Sidney Carline, Gill with his Rossall School Memorial was cited by P.G. Konody in *The Observer* as "the hero of this year's exhibition", noting that the work was "one of those rare instances of present-day religious art that carry the conviction of sincere faith and exhaltation" (30.10.27).

London was obviously a necessity, not only for Gill, but for all his friends who were engaged in similar activities. In London there were customers for stone work, galleries and dealers, those agents of the fine art market with whom, however much he detested the whole commercialized system, Gill was more than ready to do business. There was also the stimulus of lectures, meetings, and other less formal platforms for ideas. On 1 December Gill gave a lecture on 'The Future of Sculpture' at the Victoria and Albert Museum in which he reiterated the idea that architecture and sculpture had no longer anything to do with one another although this position does not seem to have deterred Gill from accepting, in the ensuing years, commissions to add rather fussy sculptural embellishments to rather plain modern buildings. In this lecture Gill also stated that the immediate future of sculpture was the museum but that "man will undoubtedly return to a new beginning" by which he meant, of course, a religious rebirth. The event was crowded and as the reviewer of the Allahabad *Pioneer* noted, it was "partly a lecture and partly a series of amusing and illuminating comments on limelight pictures of the sculpture of many periods". Gill contended that the "great religions of the world have always resulted in great artistic creation because they have helped to free man from himself"; as the reviewer of *The Pioneer* noted,

> the last half of the lecture was given in a dim light so that the audience could continue to admire the last slide, the head of a massive statue of Vishnu. 'That,' said Mr. Gill, 'is my idea of sculpture'. (31.12.27).

On 21 December Gill returned to Capel for Christmas and the New Year. Perhaps, after the ease and agreeable society of London in the previous months, the fact that he arrived "v. late owing to fog & had to walk owing to icy roads" (D 21.12.27) was of sufficient inconvenience to contribute to his realization that Capel, which had been a difficult venture in the first place, was now beginning to seem impossible. There had been the departure of his eldest daughter and also growing domestic grumblings caused by the difficult conditions and also, no doubt, by Gill's own increased absences.

Gill began work on *The Canterbury Tales*, his next project for the Golden Cockerel Press. There was music practice and Gill made a small book of engravings for Denis Tegetmeier. On Christmas Day there were midnight and morning Masses and letters and presents and cards all the morning and afternoon. For this, their last Christmas at Capel-y-ffin, Gill records that they were "snowed up" (25.12.27) and, significantly, he left Capel only four days into the New Year, not to return until mid-March.

10. David Jones: Painting in Wales and the South of France 1924-8

David Jones came to Capel very much under the influence of the Gill aesthetic which he had been absorbing during the previous years at Ditchling. However, during the period 1924 to 1928 Jones used, in quiet conjunction with his increasingly fluid manner of painting, what he had learnt from recent continental developments in art; and he took a significant step forward in the evolution of his individual and unmistakable style of working in watercolours. As John Rothenstein records, Jones maintained that it was during this period that he "began to have some idea of what" he "would ask a painting to be" (JR MEP I-M 30). Gill's continuing influence, which is evident in some of the engravings of this period, is largely absent from the paintings although there are exceptions. In the small, luminous watercolour of 1927 *St. Gregory*, Gillian mannerisms are indeed obvious though there is an expressiveness in the drawing of the nudes which is not usually to be found in Gill's own work, and there is an obvious variety in the inspiration that stands behind the painting. Jones is striving for a flexibility and a subtlety which is almost unconsidered by Gill. The figure of St Gregory himself is the stiffest element in the picture and his nimbus, as with those in the *Jonah* engravings, weakens the design.

The other painted works which most obviously register some continuing affiliation to Gill's medieval mannerisms are the tabernacle that Jones painted for the altar of the Chapel at Capel-y-ffin and the large 4'x6' painting of a crucifixion that Jones executed on the wall of the monastery. Sadly, this work cannot be lifted off the wall for much-needed preservation because it was painted on whitewash. In its present condition it has severely deteriorated and is difficult to discern, but to judge from the wavy yellow hair, the red of the spear wound, and the intense blue of the elegantly formed loincloth, the work would have been vividly coloured. The face of Christ is expressive given its stylization and the slight thinning of the limbs perhaps owes something to the proportions to be found in Gill's crucifixes where Christ tends to have long, narrow limbs. This work, along with the metal tabernacle which is also in a deteriorating condition, also give us two early examples of Jones's creative use of lettering, an art form that he was to practise and evolve in earnest towards the end of his life.

At this time Jones made a series of boxwood carvings, some of which might well have originated with discarded wood-engraving blocks and were not intended for sale. René Hague remembers a crucifixion some three inches square as being a "fine example" of Jones's work in this medium. Gill, perhaps over-affectionately, wrote that these carvings "alone would place" Jones "in the first rank of modern artists" (ARTW 23).

The important painting work that Jones did at Capel was landscape. I propose to discuss a handful of the less well-known works and to concentrate particularly on those that I am able to reproduce. Jones brought with him to Capel an often comforting *faux-naif* manner of formalizing landscape which both objectified it and tamed it. In an early Capel landscape there is an obvious attempt at formal elegance in the bold and decided contouring — the curve of a hill becomes a hedge which becomes a path which becomes a tree trunk which becomes a stump; the sweep of the line is continued with a sophisticated ingenuity. Shading confirms our expectation of shape and clouds are given a formal consonance with the contours of the hills and the whole has a meticulous and pleasant organization that was to be forsaken in the frenetic glancings of certain later Capel landscapes. Dividing the two approaches is the development of a greater sensitivity to the emotional charge of a particular subject. Jones's style becomes looser and apparently more tentative, camouflaging its formal sophistication in order to express the spiritual nuances and implications as well as the "broken contours" (RQ 4) of the Ewyas valley.

An unsettled atmosphere is immediately visible in a painting of the monastery made in February 1925, shortly after Jones's arrival at Capel-y-ffin. Perhaps the most remarkable aspect of this

16. 'Capel-y-ffin', 1925

intelligently organized work is the rhythmic complexity created by the clever articulation of buildings, branches and hills in the upper right hand corner. This knotty area is clearly significant, a feeling intensified by the termination of the right hand fork of the split path in the dark ominous doorway, a feature also present at the extreme right of a fine watercolour Jones made of Bristol docks a year later. Perhaps the painter is insecure about the uncertainties of his future and his relation to religion; questions of money and marriage were preoccupying Jones at this time and significantly and somewhat similarly the split path beside the lovers in the excellent oil *The Garden Enclosed*, made at Ditchling the year before, had not led to the doorway of the house in the background but somewhat obtusely to its corner. More dramatically, the subject of the vital *Garden Path, Ditchling* led to an abrupt termination in the centre of that work. The treatment of the trees in these earlier paintings and in Capel-y-ffin is not unrelated and certainly a sense of dramatic movement (biographical and psychological no less than formal) is set up in the rhythms on the right hand side of this view of the monastery. The eye is carried into the charged area where turmoil is somewhat arrested by the strongly defined architecture of the monastery.

Made in the first months of his first visit to Capel (December 1924-March 1925) are a series of watercolours focused on the Nant-y-Bwch of which the most resolved and well-known is *Tir Y Blaenau* in the National Library of Wales, Aberystwyth. Here the landscape is stressed; the bulk of the mountains presses the river down to the bottom of the paper and everything appears in a state of flux as if some geological upheaval is taking place. Only the grazing animals check the disturbance of the scene which gives the impression of pressing in on the viewer. Other paintings in the same series are spontaneous and playful, little more than sketches. The line which carries the rhythm dominates, these works and the colours — burnt sienna, prussian blue, black and mustard — a favourite range for Jones, are added as accents. Just as *Tir Y Blaenau* revealed the stressed nature of the landscape so the spontaneity of these others reflects the seemingly *ad hoc* nature of the scene which had been irregularly and arbitrarily rucked-up and worn down.

In his work around Capel-y-ffin Jones dramatizes the already formidable landscape just as he sometimes exoticizes the vegetation. Likewise, he enlarges the size of the two small rivers, the Nant-y-Bwch and the Honddu. These streams could be impressive; in that oddly intrusive, directly autobiographical passage of *In Parenthesis* (disclosed by the impersonal mode of 'you' for 'I'), Jones wrote: "The water in the trench-drain ran as fast as stream in Nant Honddu in the early months, when you go to get the milk from Pen-y-Maes" (IP 77). Except in early spring the streams are little more than brooks, yet in a work like *Pasture by Water* (1926) we see the stream in full flood, scooping and bouncing over submerged stones. This painting is unusual in its utilization of perspective space; it has a depth though the vertical branches of the trees sweep the eye upwards giving the feeling of a steep incline to the hill, and these two contrary motions pull the composition apart in a rather disturbing manner. The sense of movement is ubiquitous; even the disposition of the grazing sheep on the page reflects the cascading motion of the water. The fact that the paint appears to have been slapped on and that curious incidentals are given heavy accents further disturbs the spectator's eye. Jones shows himself, in the most free of these landscapes, as a shy or timid expressionist. Gill drew attention to this freedom in the notes that he wrote in 1928 in preparation for Jones's first one-man exhibition: "Some critics have complained that, whereas his wood-engravings are overlaboured and tight, his water colours are unfinished and loose" (NLW 1978 dep 111). When one begins to study one of these watercolours the looseness is never shallow or disorganized but is rather the palpitation of a submerged expressionism. Beneath their surface delicacy Jones's paintings are often stressed and in the more disturbed works he seems to violate space with aggressive, almost meaningless marks that tend towards a kind of automatic writing.

The fact that paintings appear unfinished also derives from the fact that the watercolour was often applied thinly and sparingly. Apart from aesthetic motives, Petra Tegetmeier recalled that Jones thinned his paint in order to economize (CON). While this may or may not be true it is quite probable that Jones used poor quality cheap paint. Pictures kept in portfolios have, over the the years, retained a depth of colour while those exposed to the light have paled considerably.

At Capel-y-ffin Jones again became interested in animal drawing which had been a preoccupation and which had resulted in

17. 'Pasture by Water', 1926

such remarkable drawing and painting when he was a young child. Around Capel "those small, wiry, hardy, shaggy but graceful, long maned ponies" with their "Arabian strain" (LC 44) fascinated Jones. These appear in a good number of the drawings and watercolours, their forms sometimes reflecting forms in the landscape as in *Hill Pastures Capel-y-ffin*. During this period Jones also made numerous studies of pigs, horses, goats and other animals which, Hills suggests, "formed the basis for the engravings to the *Chester Play of the Deluge* "(TG 84) in which the animals are skilfully and elegantly articulated — anything but 'overlaboured' though 'tight' in the best possible sense.

As well as more serious work done at Capel there was work in a lighter vein reflecting the atmosphere of fun that counterpointed the serious artistic dedication and religious devotion. Denis Tegetmeier was depicted in a quasi-cartoon linear style engaged in one of his tasks about the monastery, the drowning of kittens (*VNVS HOMO PER AQUAM NOBIS RESTITVIT REM*). In another cartoon Jones records an incident which he took as marking the beginning of his lifelong friendship with the printer, translator and exegete of Jones's own difficult poetry, René Hague. In '*DVO HOMINES PER AQVAM NOBIS RESTITVERVNT REM*' Jones is self-satirically seen watching while somebody else does the work. As most witnesses recall, Jones wasn't disposed to help much about the place; while others did it, Jones drew it. *DVO HOMINES*, with its mock-heroic title, recalls the incident on Christmas Eve 1924, two days after Jones first arrived at Capel, when Hague went to unblock a mountain stream to restore the house's water supply. But the image of freeing the waters to insure fertility, which Jones later uses in *In Parenthesis* (p 84) and in *The Anathemata* (pp. 225-7 & 238), is a theme in Aryan literature that is first encountered as far back as the ancient *Rig Veda* where Indra claimed, "For all mankind I set the rivers free" (RR 29). *DVO HOMINES* was not drawn until 1928 and marks the fact that by that date Jones had begun to place a great importance on his friendship with René Hague. As with his association with Harman Grisewood and Eric Gill, friendship with Hague constituted, for Jones, an intellectual freeing of the waters. In 1928 it was Hague to whom Jones showed his first attempts at what was to become *In Parenthesis* and throughout his life he had recourse to René Hague on questions of classical and

18. 'DVO HOMINES PER AQVAM NOBIS RESTITVERVNT'

medieval literature.

One particularly interesting drawing and watercolour of 1926 is *Blaeu Bwch*, which possesses a tapestry-like quality that derives from a combination of differing and juxtaposed textures and a Cézanne-like compartmentalization of the landscape; indeed, the top left hand corner of the painting appears to owe something directly to that artist. *Blaeu Bwch* is a strange, original and daring composition in which there is a considerable flattening of the landscape, so much so, in fact, that the stream appears to run almost vertically. The over-large, out-of-scale, mid-ground trees also compromise perspectival space and there is, furthermore, a playful spatial complication in the bottom left hand corner where a cow appears to float in the air, or at the very least, to bestride a large chasm.

In the oft-reproduced *Y Twmpa* we see Jones's extensive use of texturing with the pencil. This is not just the technique of some-one who was also an engraver but reflects the fact that the land-scape around Capel gives the impression of being multi-textured as it is a mixture of pasture, scrub, rock and wood. And to stress the fact that this was a period of exciting experimentation for Jones, we should note that there is another treatment of *Y Twmpa* where texture is nothing and, by contrast, colour is used to dramatize the form. This colour is applied in broad, bold areas and daubs, heightened and unrealistic, recalling in a softer mode the experiments of the *Fauves* or *Die Brücke* artists. Jones made similar experiments in garish, unrealistic colour on Caldey where much of the paper was left white and the results appear to be studies for the pronounced stratifications of the rock forms in a finished work such as *Bay on Caldey*.

The penultimate work of the Capel period that I wish to con-sider is *The Honddu Fach River, June* (1926) which is intense and alarming, a truly sub-expressionist landscape. Again, though here on a more intimate scale, there is a feeling that the terrain has been crushed together and only the mundanity in the draw-ing of the bridge and fence anchors the spectator amid the fluid and dislocating ructions and the sense of gusting. Again this landscape is divided up into sections but here the feeling is not so much of intricate tapestry but of the clippings of collage where one element cuts across another. It is a charged work by a man whose eyes, to recall Rothenstein's words, "had in their depths a

19. 'Blaeu Bwch', 1926

20. 'The Honddu Fach River, June', 1926

little touch of fanaticism".

Lastly, the work that appears on the cover of this book, *Hill Pastures Capel-y-ffin*, is a work that Gill considered to be the "best of a group of mountain landscapes made in 1926 and the previous year" (JR MEP I-M 289). Despite the obtrusive flowers near the bottom left hand corner which are drawn like those first created in his childhood drawings and which persist in Jones's late mythological paintings (e.g. *Y Cyfarchiad I Fair*), the work is strong and demonstrates Jones's response to the powerful rhythms which he discerned in the local landscape. Again there is variety in the texturing and the colours are subdued — tawny, greeny browns, almost the colour of camouflage. A lone house winks like some cheeky cubist or Chagallian intrusion from beneath the curve of the hill which slices it.

During the years that he visited Capel-y-ffin, Jones also painted much in Brockley, some in Bristol when he stayed with Douglas Cleverdon, some at Waltham St Lawrence when visiting the Gibbings and at Portslade on the south coast. The styles of paintings made in each locality differ as Jones was becoming sensitive to site, an important concept in his later thinking and writing. During these years, through his process of ceaseless exploration, Jones shed certain earlier mannerisms while adopting others. The years 1924 to 1928 marked the beginning of that astoundingly prolific period of his life in which Jones was at his most painterly and which was abruptly terminated by his first major breakdown in 1932.

Caldey Island

In March 1925 Jones went from Gill's erstwhile monastery at Capel-y-ffin to the real monastery on Caldey where he developed, over a series of visits, his talents as a seascapist. Before he left for his first trip to Caldey he had begun to engrave *Gulliver's Travels*, but as he wrote to Philip Hagreen, "Gulliver or no Gulliver I must take the opportunity and do some outdoor work" (DG 34). Caldey is, for the most part, a rather flat island but what Jones responded to was "the murderously sharp rocks" along its coast (DG 34). You can see Jones marking the forms of these cliffs in those garishly coloured studies to which I referred above. There are affinities in Jones's Caldey paintings with work by artists like Ben Nicholson, Christopher Wood and Paul Nash and there are also, and probably unbeknown to Jones, similarities, in certain treatments of the rock folds, to early twentieth century American artists such as Arthur Dove and Georgia O'Keefe.

In certain works there persists the tendency to formalize and conceptualize. And as Jones is keen to mark the wriggling contour of the coast and as he is reluctant to register depth, the line of the rocks sometimes curves flatly up the page seeming disconcertingly like the profile formed by jig-saw pieces. Because of this habit of flattening, when Tenby appears (as in *Vessels Sheltering* 1927) it appears closer than it actually is.

The bulk of Jones's work on Caldey focused on the numerous bays and tackled the problem of the sea. He wrote to Philip Hagreen: "it is difficult not be led up various impressionistic and realistic and otherwise dangerous paths when faced with the sea — or — even worse, to fall back on some dead convention" (DG 34). The result of this wrangle is uneven but, as is becoming apparent in this survey of even a part of a short period of Jones's life, he was always trying different ways to solve a creative problem. One of the most difficult aspects of painting the sea is that it is something that we perceive in a state of constant motion; Jones sought, even in static subjects, a quality of movement and his seas often shimmer or trouble according to the mood of the work. The sea was of enormous significance for Jones and it was during these years at Caldey and at Portslade on the Sussex coast that he was able to spend much time studying it.

On Caldey Jones was among friends from Capel such as Dom Theodore Bailey and he was able to work, when he wanted, indoors in the scriptorium. What he found, in fact, was another home away from home, an agreeable and sympathetic haven in which to work while being sheltered from the vicissitudes of the everyday world. The first trip he made was of three months duration which was as long as his first stay at Capel and he returned to the island for a week in mid-August of the same year. The next stay of any length was made in October 1927. On that occasion he wrote to H.S. Ede that "I have had pretty good weather — *no* interesting results of attempts at painting yet — getting rather worn by trying and failing" (27.10.27 KYC). It is typical of Jones's humility and severe self-critical faculty to designate his work as "attempts". After the trip he wrote again to Ede:

21. 'The Wave', 1927

> I did an immense amount of tearing up at Caldey but one or two of
> the remaining ones I myself like — & indeed think them in a curious
> way the best things I have done so far.*
> * This is probably rubbish — some of them are awful (4.11.27 KYC).

This sort of vacillating indecision is surely indicative of an artist
in a process of exploration and experimentation.

One work made during this trip was *The Wave*. The composition is an odd one for Jones; most Caldey views are content to use
the cup shape of the bay but here we see a blunt vertical cliff and
rocks jutting out against a troubled sea with a wave scooping to
break in the foreground. Apart from its singularity, what is mar-
vellous about this watercolour and gouache is the variety of ways
in which Jones creates the movement of the sea; there are washes,
scumbling, rubbed dry paint, fine pencil lines, squiggles, blobs
and jabs. Above the sea, clouds created with gouache and clusters
of parallel lines in pencil echo the water's uneasy motion. Against
the sea the delicately delineated form of the wave arches towards
the beach. The rather ugly shapes and relations of the major
compositional elements of cliff, pinnacle, horizon line and wave
are modulated by the nuances of light, shadow and other less
explicable accenting. The painting is charged with that sense of
latent mystery that is to be found in Jones's best work. The halo
of light about the pinnacle rock gives it a quasi-magical charge
without sacrificing its spontaneously observed quality. Indeed
Caldey must have appeared to Jones as something of an enchanted
place. In *Tenby from Caldey Island* (1925) Jones responded to the
mysterious magical aspect of some dark woods on the island.
Increasingly, overt preoccupation with formality was being dis-
placed by growing sensitivity to atmosphere and metaphysical
intimation.

Salies de Béarn

Jones painted a large number of watercolours looking out from
the *Villa des Palmiers* where he was staying with the Gills in
Salies de Béarn in 1928. These were painted from the verandah
or from a window, a sheltered position like that so often chosen
not only by Jones himself but by one of his favourite contemporary artists, Bonnard. The warmth and light of the south of

France do not appear to have made much impact on the mood of Jones's painting as frenetic and unsettling elements are still evident. The artist may at times have tried to suppress this sense of disturbance but it is ever manifest in the speedy execution and in the random and neurotic accentings of unlikely features. As time went by the artist's colours and markings seemed less and less to inhabit the objects that they help describe; they become more abstractly expressive not so much of something seen but of something felt. The question of the relationship of a Jones painting to the place in which it was made is tricky and was partly expressed by Eric Gill in his article on David Jones in *Artwork*:

> Though in one place he may find more inspiration than another, it is not places that concern him. What concerns him is the universal thing showing through the particular thing, and as a painter it is this showing through that he endeavours to capture (ARTW 23 177).

Yet, at the same time, Jones was becoming increasingly sensitive to the importance of site to culture; implicitly, discreetly perhaps, Jones is more conscious of site and locality than Gill ever was. However it is true to say that Jones's visual inclination is indeed to move away from what he actually beholds. Gill wrote about Jones in 1928 that he

> saw that the substance of a work of art was an intellectual construction and not a similitude — it was realistic and representational only by accident (NLW III 27).

Add to that neo-Thomist explanation the notion that in the Romantic or in the expressionist tradition a scene acts as a vehicle for emotion and then we can adequately approach Jones's work.

In *Landscape at Salies de Béarn,* painted from the verandah of the *Villa des Palmiers* one is conscious of Jones's wish to exploit to the full the expressive potential of watercolour. The landscape vibrates under the energetic application of the paint, a house is surrounded with deep colour and appears curiously ghosted, and a frond is heavily weighted with colour; all sense of 'reality' is subordinated to Jones's swift expressive experiments with this medium.

Not so far away from Salies is the shrine at Lourdes which was a source of consternation for Jones, and the gouache that now

147

22. 'Landscape at Salies de Béarn', 1928

hangs in Kettle's Yard, Cambridge appears almost silly, an essay in *faux-naif* that evokes little more than the toytown aspect of the place. The hills about Lourdes gave rise to craggier or frillier landscape effects than those at Capel. These hills are seen more panoramically and do not appear to possess the same bulking heaviness of their Breconshire counterparts. Paul Hills has noted that in works like *River Gave in the Pyrenees* and *Montes et Omnes Colles* shadows are created, as in Bonnard's work, by contrasts of colour and that colour is therefore freed from its task of describing shadow to work in an experimental manner (TG 44); this is certainly true of *Montes et Omnes Colles* with its strong meandering rhythm and its variety of foci. In *River Gave in the Pyrenees*, however, the accents seem insufficiently pointed and the whole appears to be rather flimsy.

In a work like *Roman Land*, painted near Lourdes, Jones builds up depth while losing none of his spontaneous energy. There is scumbling, paint thickened, paint thinned, smudged dry colour — all creating an exciting variety of effects. Block out the Napoleonic Barracks and the landscape vibrates; Jones sadly appears to have needed to utilize such anchors and when he frees himself (such as in *The Legion's Ridge* of 1946) he reveals a courage and a power that he so often mistakenly suppresses.

Whether in their subtle and intelligent use of the recent developments in modern art or in the energy and originality of their sub-expressionism, the best works done in this short but important period of Jones's development as a painter mark the maturation of a man who had a remarkable visual perception and who, while being susceptible to outside influence, was quick to assimilate and develop such influence. By the mid-1920s Jones had struck out and had begun to explore his own independent and unique range.

11. 1928 'Their green valleys lead nowhere'

Gill spent the latter half of 1 January sorting prints, mounting them and making a list of engravings for the selection to be published in book form by Douglas Cleverdon. Back in London a few days later he saw Cleverdon at supper with Stanley Morison and again several days later with David Jones when Cleverdon stayed late to discuss their project. The month was characterized by a great deal of social activity. Gill saw a lot of Jones and shared in Jones's dual focus: firstly on the Chelsea circle of Catholic intelligentsia which centred itself around the Burns's house in St Leonard's Terrace and secondly on H.S. Ede's house in Hampstead where the more cosmopolitan gatherings were devoted to the world of modern art and where, on one occasion, Jones met Georges Braque.

At the end of the month Gill was beginning to work on an essay that criticized the kitsch of repository art and which was to be published by Tom Burns in *Order*. He also wrote to his daughter Joanna noting that

> This London adventure is nearly over now.... If the show is a success one may be able to afford something in the way of six months drawing in Paris for you (31.1.28 WAC).

Gill noted that his sculpting was progressing favourably and that the big figure that was to be called *Mankind* and was to be the centre piece of the forthcoming show "is good in parts".

Early in February Gill made a short trip to Bradford to see Fr. John O'Connor. There he began writing a lecture on 'Art and Prudence' and then went on to Liverpool to see his brother. Back in London he went to an exhibition of Henry Moore sculptures and then on to a 7 & 5 Society show where he met his daughter Joanna and David Jones who remembered these as "the gayest and most varied in London" (TG 34).

The 7 & 5 Society to which Jones was elected as a member in 1928 had been founded eight years earlier as a non-partisan exhibiting society. Its first catalogue proclaimed that "Individual members have their own theories of Art, but as a group the SEVEN & FIVE has none". Certainly, the widely differing styles of the members (which by 1928 included among others Ivon Hitchens, Sidney Hunt, Cedric Morris, Ben and Winifred Nicholson, Edward Wolfe and Christopher Wood) supports this assertion. However, despite stylistic differences, H.S. Ede did perceive in their 1926 exhibition a common "light and airy" feeling about all their work, just as later Alan Bowness discerned a common "lyrical quality" (MG 7&5 SC). By 1926 Glazebrook suggests that they had become the "most progressive exhibiting society in London" (MG 7&5 SC) but increasingly they were to become a forum for the abstract tendencies of Ben Nicholson who became chairman in that year. This growing focus on abstraction explains why Jones's association with them became more tenuous in the early part of the next decade until he was 'voted out' of the society in 1933.

For the forthcoming Goupil show Gill had been persuaded to carve 'on spec' whereas normally his carvings were "'jobs'. . . undertaken for a specific purpose" (DC EEG xii). It was this unusual procedure that had necessitated his working in London though earlier works such as the *Portland Stone Crucifix* and the *Caryatid* were included among the fifteen sculptures and twenty-four drawings exhibited at the Goupil gallery in March. The star attraction was the Hoptonwood kneeling torso *Mankind*, which Gill and Cribb had carved at Glebe Place during the previous months. This attracted much attention and the show made Gill something of a celebrity. Pages of photos of his work appeared both in *The London Illustrated News* and in *The Sphere* and R.H. Wilenski wrote in *Apollo* that the exhibition left people "'waiting for the next phase of this artist's development with quickened interest and some impatience" (28 May 206-12). For *Mankind* Gill received the impressive sum of £800 which was to prove very useful when the expense of buying, repairing and moving to a new home occurred later in the year.

Gill's enjoyment of his prolonged stay in London certainly seemed to have quickened his ideas about quitting Capel. Writing to Desmond Chute, he recorded:

> It *was* a go! I enjoyed it v. much really & Glebe Place became quite a 'home from Home'. Mary & the girls visited me from time to time — seems like a dream to look back on. C-y-ff is v. heavenly — but...whether we stay...remains to be seen.(LET 229,

During March Gill was off around the country: to Waltham St Lawrence; to Hawkesyard where Fr. O'Connor was preaching and where Gill enjoyed a sing-song with the novices; to Bradford; to Liverpool; to Preston; and to Bristol to discuss the engravings book with Douglas Cleverdon yet again before he returned to Capel for his wife's birthday on 14 March. The rest of the month was spent at the monastery working on *sans serif* numerals for Stanley Morison, finishing the essay on 'Art and Prudence' and finishing some life drawings. On 24 March a telegram arrived from his eldest daughter Betty to say that a son, who must have been conceived almost as soon as she was married, had been born.

In early April Gill was reading *The Canterbury Tales* which was his next Golden Cockerel project. Cleverdon visited to sort prints on 10 April and afterwards Gill was off to London via Birmingham to rejoin Mary who had been staying with Elizabeth at Ditchling since the birth of their grandchild. In London on 13 April Gill visited the Tate with his wife and with David Jones and they all went, that night, to the Old Vic to see *A School for Scandal*.

The next evening they met David Jones and Robert Gibbings at Victoria and set off to France. For David Jones it was the first time that he had crossed the channel since the war and while this trip was to be pacific it is interesting to note that after his return he began his "experiment in writing" concerned with the western front, *In Parenthesis*.

The party stayed in Paris. The Edes were also there and they lunched together after which Jones spent the rest of the afternoon with them while Gill, Mary and Robert Gibbings walked round the *Ile de la cité* and later met Zadkine. The following day there was an outing to Chartres. Whereas Gill was moved by the deeply mysterious late twelfth century cathedral with its exciting carvings and its glorious stained glass windows, Jones enraged Gill by preferring the rather damp, uncluttered and austere light-stoned church of St Pierre. Their dispute on this subject continued to occupy them on their long overnight journey to Salies. Blissett was later told by Jones that "A little boy with them on the train, when asked by his parents, who met him, how he had slept, said that the lady was very nice and quiet but that the two gentlemen had argued all night" (LC 17).

The Gills and Jones were met by Gordian but the long dispute had obviously taken its toll: they rested in the afternoon of 17 April, were up late the next morning and showed David Jones the town in the afternoon. Gordian, who was generally happy at his French school, was glad to see his parents; he had written rather poignantly that "i am very very glad that you are coming here...it is a long time that i have not seen you is it not" — French constructions were obviously disrupting his ear for English syntax. He sweetly went on to say that "i am a fraid that i coud not send enny thing big for your birthday, hear are som violets from our garden".

As David Jones was deeply affected by the Welsh tradition of heroic defeat, so he was impressed to find himself in the country that was the setting for the *Chanson du Roland*. As he put it in a lament for the dead towards the end of *In Parenthesis,*

> And in the country of Béarn — Oliver
> and all the rest - so many without momento
> beneath the tumuli on the high hills
> and under the harvest places (IP 163).

In a note to that passage he acknowledges that while Roncesvalles is not strictly in the Béarn country (it is actually just over the border in Spain), he states that his hostess had informed him that a gap that he could see in the hills from the window of the *Villa des Palmiers* "was indeed the pass where Roland fell" (IP n. 221-2). Jones made a simple landscape in Salies which he entitled *Roland's Tree* to mark the association; before he dared to include historical incident in his mature work, Jones developed the habit of choosing titles that marked an historic association. Jones was also aware of the influence of the Romans in this part of the world. While Gill in his *Autobiography* found an ox-drawn wagon that he saw at Salies to be "a heraldic symbol of that good life" (AUT 237), Jones found an ox-drawn plough which he saw outside nearby Lourdes to be something that "seemed to sum up the whole feeling of France as part of the 'imperium' " (BCT) and therefore he called the landscape he painted which included these oxen, *Roman Land.*

During this visit to Salies Gill did a lot of drawing around the town, worked on an article called 'The Criterion in Art' for *The Dublin Review* and did some work on the *sans serif* type face for the Monotype Corporation. Much time was spent enjoying French café life at Lousteau's Café Central ("Repas 2f"). One day Gill, Mary, Gordian, Elizabeth Bill and David Jones went to Lourdes by car and visited the Grotto and churches and said vespers. Afterwards they visited the Hagreens who were living, as Jones put it, in a "little house...just outside the enclosure of a convent of Dominican nuns — who sing the office with a more marvelous beauty than I have before heard" (DG 45-6). After the Gills set off back to England on 4 May, Jones went to stay with the Hagreens.

The landscape around Lourdes is, as Jones so aptly described it in a letter to H.S. Ede, "awfully panoramic" and the weather was wet and the snowy mountains began to appear to Jones, not so much as rocky bulks, but "as kind of lights hung in the sky", going on to note that he hadn't yet learnt to paint the effect (21.5.28 KYC). The "ghastly commercialism" of the town itself clearly disturbed him; "it's like finding a Woolworth store on the summit of The Mount of Olives" (21.5.28 KYC). Perhaps this aversion coupled with his dislike of panoramic subjects led him to sound that note of despair that later became so familiar: "I should like to get more work done before I do return. I've done so many utter duds — it's so exhausting & depressing" (21.5.28 KYC). Before going back to England, Jones went with the Hagreens to visit the bourgeois resort of Arcachon with its fantastic gingerbread villas and Jones painted the bay.

Gill and his wife had meanwhile returned to Paris where they met Robert Gibbings and where Gill drew at the Chaumière. Although Gill had written to R.A. Walker from Salies that "urgent work awaits my attention at Capel-y-ffin" (3.5.28 WAC), he and his wife stopped in London on 8 May when a singular but perhaps unsurprising entry occurs in Gill's diary: "to Pimlico with MEG — house hunting". An entry not surprising when one considers that the year was five and a quarter months old and Gill had spent only thirty-two days of it at Capel. Betty's marriage and move to Sussex followed by the removal of the Att-waters to Machynlleth in central Wales meant that the running of the establishment at Capel-y-ffin entailed a punishing increase in the work load for those remaining. And perhaps the final event that precipitated the decision to abandon Capel was that the ailing Fr. Woodford was ordered to Switzerland for reasons of health and this meant that there would be no Mass within fifteen miles of the monastery. Furthermore the buildings, despite the efforts of the previous four years, were in a bad state of repair. From the point of view of work Gill had found the local stone difficult to carve and anything larger than a small sculpture almost impossible to transport.

Gill spent six days from 9 to 15 May at Capel finishing some drawings made in Salies and Paris before going on the familiar round to Bristol to see Cleverdon about the engraving book, to Waltham St Lawrence to visit the Golden Cockerel Press and then to London to visit the Goupil Gallery about his drawings. The period from 19 May until 18 June was spent back at Capel in a bout of concentrated work in which Gill began seriously drawing and engraving his designs for *The Canterbury Tales*. At this same time, Denis Tegetmeier discovered Pigotts Farm near High Wycombe and considered that it promised to be a viable alternative to Capel; when Gill made a brief trip to London on 18 June, Tegetmeier took Mary Gill to see it.

In mid-June David Jones wrote to Douglas Cleverdon: "*I have returned* ... I forthwith proceed with Mariner. I was working violently in France trying to get watercolours done for a show I hope to have in the autumn' (DC DJE 16). Jones began the task of making about 150 to 200 preliminary drawings for the eight copperplate engravings and two vignettes that were to grace his edition of Coleridge's *Rime of the Ancient Mariner*. He also began to consider doing "a lot of illustrations with long 'captions' of a sort" (Let 27.4.62 NLW 1978 Dep II/4 2) on the subject of his experiences in the trenches. This rapidly developed into "an attempt to see how this business of 'form' & 'content' worked in a *writing* as compared with the same problems in...the visual arts" (Let Miss Jones 20.8.68 NLW 1978 Dep II/14). This 'attempt' was to pre-

occupy Jones for the next four years, a period of prodigious output in watercolour and words. Jones sent an early draft (perhaps
even the very first) of the beginning of the work to René Hague
who became not only a constant adviser but also the printer when
Faber's published the work in 1937:

>   To Mr René Hague
> Private Leg sick — Private Ball absent
> 01 Ball, 01 Ball, Ball of No 4
> where's Ball-25201 Ball — you
> Corporal he's in your section
> ....
> Movement round and about the commanding officer
> "Bugler — will you sound Orderly Sergeants".....
> a hurrying of feet from three companys
> converging on a little group apart
> where on horses sit the Central Command.
> But from B Company there is no such
> darting out — the Orderly Sergeant of B
> is licking the stub-end of his lead pencil
> — it divides a little his
> fairish, moist, moustache.
> Heavily jolting and sideways jostling — the
> noise of liquid shaken in some small
> vessell by a regular jogging movement
> and certain clinking ending in a scuffling
> and a scraping of feet side long — all
> clear and distinct in that singular silence
> peculiar to parade grounds and to Refectories
> where are monks — the silence
> of an high order, full of peril in the
> breaking of it — like the coming on parade
> of John Ball.
> He settles down between number 4 and 5 of
> the rear rank — "Here sergeant"
> *I've* been here a long time Pte. Ball!!
> "Have that man's name taken if you please Mr. Jenkins"
> "Take that man's name Sergeant Snell"
> "Take 'is name Corporal
> late on parade, the Batt'on being
> paraded for overseas — 'ave you got
> his name Corporal — 'is name &
> his number—"
> Pte. Bum nudged Pte Wastebottom, They've
> took Balls' name & number —
> I know — I 'erd 'em.
> Pte Ball's pack, ill adjusted & formless

hangs a little more heavily on his shoulder blades
his spirit sickened
and retired within itself.
For when the bludgeoning of chance becomes
too unspeakable,the brain in self-defence
just floats unsteered wherever it may choose
— how it tacks and veers — John Ball
forgot the iniquity of those in high places
and considered many things in them selves
wholly unconnected — He started off with
the white porch of his home —
and the Palatinus then veered into
better verse — "the Gentlemen of England now abed"
— abed A-bed Beds in general
& once the brain gets hold of the
idea *bed* the narrow straits of
the contingent are passed and one enters
the vast limitless ocean of
an idea — from Corporal Spragler's
favourite post-cards to St. John the Apostle
or John the Elder is it
— & the beds the saints rejoice in:
— then this business of the Gospels
— odd texts floated about — Centurians —
— they had charge of a hundred men
like Captain Aubrey Trubshaw, — there —
on his nice horse
— at this point he noticed the excellent
profile of Mr. Jenkins & all his
elegance — like
a gentleman of Verona — with yellow hair:
Paolo Ucello — The Rout of San Romano
the squire with the profile and the yellow hair
all unhelmeted — the Rout of San Romano
— we don't have lances now — nor banners
nor trumpets, at least not respectable
trumpets — I wonder if they blew
'Defaulters' on the Ucello
Trumpets —
we have horses — but not war horses
really — no — Ucello — 14 something
— 14 something or other — *Gunpowde*r —
yes thats it, gunpowder —
that "a little altered things"
as Browning says but it must
be more than that —
Pte Ball reajusted his pack with one hand
God! no mess-tin cover, (NLW).

The "refectories" and "monks" are immediate memories of Caldey and these seem eventually to have been transmuted into the spiritual figure of Aneurin Merddyn Lewis who "brings in a manner, baptism,and metaphysical order to the bankruptcy of the occasion" (IP 2). Privates Bum and Wastebottom were expressive jokes and Wastebottom was retained; in Part 7 of the finished book we find that "he married a wife on his Draft-leave but the whinnying splinter razored diagonal and mess-tin fragments drove inward and toxined underwear" (IP 157-8) — an appropriate end for someone whose name characterizes the wasting of a generation not held by the cosmocrats, to be of sufficient value to be allowed life. At any rate, comparison of the draft I have quoted with the first pages of *In Parenthesis* shows what a powerful and inspired beginning Jones had made to a new and even more important career as a poet.

On 26 June Gill went to Oxford where he looked at the Piero della Francesca in Christchurch before going on to Waltham St Lawrence. On the next day Gibbings drove Gill and Joanna to Pigotts Farm which was three and a half miles north of High Wycombe and consisted of about seventeen acres in a clearing on top of a hill covered in beech woods. There was a wonderfully isolated feel about the place considering it was right in the heart of the Home Counties and therefore close to London. Two and a half weeks later Gill visited solicitors in Reading about the purchase of this property. Even though the prospect of transporting large slabs of stone up the steep hill must have seemed almost as daunting as getting the same up to Capel-y-ffin, Gill was happy to have the possibility of establishing a holy life so close to the inescapable and necessary London. He was also glad to be closer to his collaborator Robert Gibbings.

Significantly, it was only after Gill had decided to move from Capel to which he had flown in order to escape from the problems of Ditchling, that he met Hilary Pepler on 30 July, "by appointment....& discussed agreement to withdraw all claims on both sides" (D 30.7.28); the long Ditchling wrangle was to be abandoned — Gill was cutting loose from cutting loose. From a new position of, as it were, complete independence he was able, officially, to forgive and forget.

Back at Capel Gill continued to work on *The Canterbury Tales* and also on drawings for a font on Caldey which was to be carved, for the most part, by Laurie Cribb in Portland stone. This was finished on 19 September — perhaps an apt artefact with which to draw to a close his work in a monastery that had been a dependency of the Caldey monks.

On 24 September Petra and Joanna took the milk float to Llanvihangel in order to ship it off to Betty in Sussex and on 26 September packing began in earnest and continued until 10 October. On 8 October the Chapel was dismantled and two days later goodbye calls were made. On the following day the family left Capel-y-ffin by Charlie Smith's lorry at 8.10, arriving at Pigotts at 6.0 p.m.

Gill would come to look back on the best aspects of Capel-y-ffin with a degree of perhaps unintentional ambiguity:

> Let the industrial-capitalist disease do its worst — the Black Mountains of Brecon will remain untouched and their green valleys lead nowhere (AUT 229).

12. Afterword

In his *Autobiography* Eric Gill expressed a wish to "write a special book all about our four years in the Black Mountains. I did not intend ever to leave Capel. I did not anticipate any reason for doing so" (227). Capel-y-ffin had proved to be an ideal but not a very practical place to live. While Gill was able to work industriously on his frequent train journeys, he did spend a considerable amount of time during this period just travelling. And despite the quality of life at Capel, Gill realized that the demands of his work necessitated living closer to London. Pigotts promised similar qualities of insulation without the problems of isolation.

It is difficult, especially in a book that deals with only a short period of Gill's life, to present a balanced view of his work. But I hope to have celebrated his importance as a person who stood apart from the prevailing trends of society and who attacked its shortcomings. Rather than being an original thinker he was a collator and teacher and his influence in that realm was significant. On the other hand, does much of Gill's prolific visual output still merit much attention? Isolated engravings and carvings, yes; the typography certainly; and also some of the unpublished erotica. But ultimately Gill the man is more fascinating than much of his work in which he kept his stress at bay and which consequently remained impoverished and prettified. As the reviewer of the *Morning Post* noted in respect of the 1928 Goupil show, his "fine works" are "not infrequently marred by whimsical fancy" (1.3.28). David Jones by contrast would, more often than not, allow the stress of internal pressures into the arena of his painting and would consequently produce more rigorous and more complex work.

What both men shared, as Cecil Gill observed, was "a heaven-born humility" (MBEG 18.11.49), noting on another occasion that his brother "never really considered himself as an 'artist' " (CG/DK WAC). At first sight this may simply appear to relate to what Herbert Read called Gill's lifelong "protest against the distinction between the artist and the ordinary man" (ACOMC) but perhaps it also refers to Gill's own estimation of his artistic capacities. In reply to the offence taken by Epstein over some remarks that Gill made about Epstein's sculpture in *G.K.'s Weekly*, Gill suggested that Epstein could have retaliated thus:

> "I Epstein, should like to suggest that Mr Gill, even if he be a good stone carver, is an indifferent artist. He's too much interested in aesthetic theory and politics and religion to be a good artist and the Stations of the Cross in Westminster Cathedral, for instance, are in consequence very little more than a milk-and-watery mixture of Byzantinism and the Arts and Crafts." Such a letter would, I think, express the truth and would have been fair tit-for-tat (Let EPST 16.2.29 WAC).

When Gill wrote that "sham byzantine is no more to be sought after than sham gothic" (OF 14.2.27) he knew that he himself was not guiltless.

By 1928 Gill had worked himself into a complex position. Life was becoming confusing: he liked Capel but he needed London; he found himself reviewing pseudonomously in *Pax* an article that he had written anonymously in *Order*; he was writing against monopoly capitalism but publishing his attacks in expensive limited editions. In August 1928 Br. Savage, writing in the *Liverpool Daily Post* on the subject of the proposed publication of 'Art and Prudence' at seventeen shillings and sixpence noted that "wealthy collectors rather than the students who read and desire to read it are likely to capture the five hundred copies which are all that are being printed" (6.8.28). Add to such paradoxes Gill's problematic sexual drives and dilemmas and we can imagine a life becoming increasingly fraught by contradiction and conflict. In the following decade these problems persisted and David Jones suggested that Gill may have died in 1940 while he was still relatively young as a result of "despair...he may have died at the impossibility of making a kind of tolerable human world as he saw it" (BBC HRC).

Gill was an enigmatic figure with an obviously devilish (or disarmingly angelic) charm. Incestuous tendencies are often linked by psychologists to the need for secrecy or for a double life and Gill with his constant affairs seems to have needed these. Yet such desire for secrecy existed side by side with Gill the clever and eager self-publicist. He was not slow to send his writings to influential and possibly interested people, neither was he reluctant to rush into print where even an Angelic Doctor might have feared to tread. From this hunger for privacy and publicity Gill, with his considerable phallocratic energy, emerges as a kind of "priapic leader". The emphasis that he placed upon the phallus can be judged from an image that he chose to express the power of religion in which "we are f****d by Christ" (FA 26).

In an evaluation of Gill the man we have to be careful about what Gill called the "prudent man's inclination to see in the pleasures of the senses mere filthiness". Yet if one's pleasures are taken at the expense of others then some kind of violation takes place. And if incest *per se* may not necessarily be an evil perhaps the confusion of relationships to which it gives rise may prove bewildering and even damaging to the participants. In the text *In A Strange Land* Gill defined the human as someone who is "responsible for his acts and for the intended consequences of his acts" (152). When he writes elsewhere of man that "his sensuality, his silliness, always lead him astray" (AN 295), the comment is perhaps more self-critical than the innocent reader might imagine.

Gill's chief goodness was that his drive and energy were dauntless; whatever one thinks of his art work, the will of the man was enormous. He was a person who made things happen — from sexual triflings to the creation of useful homes where artists could come to learn and work. His advocacy and encouragement of the habit of art as a normal and vital part of life was both generous and helpful to others. Gill affected people's lives and David Jones commented that "I don't think that he was a great artist" but went on to say "I think he was a great man" (BBC HRC). Gill's largeness of character is why people cannot seem to let him go; movingly, Gill himself desired that on his tombstone, carved by Laurie Cribb, he should merely be described as a "Stone Carver" for he considered himself, above all, to be a worker, man the maker, purely and simply.

After the Capel period there were new apprentices, new and

larger projects, books, collected essays, new desires and increased strain and stress. What Gill found at Pigotts was described in a letter to Desmond Chute:

> a courtyard surrounded by erstwhile farm buildings — viz: two largebarns, stables etc. & a farm house & two cottages thus:-
> A Cottage for Petra and Denis T.
> B " for Laurie Cribb and family
> C " for E.G. & Co.
> D Barn for E.G.'s workshop
> FFF open sheds for future workshop
> * Future chapel
> ...and all for £1750, including 1 acre orchard and 16 acres grass (LET 237).

Pigotts provided Gill, for the last twelve years of his life, with his beloved quadrangle arrangement for his extended family in a location that was utterly secluded and yet within easy reach of the capital. Pigotts would be Capel again in a less desperate and daunting location. Capel had been a magnificent challenge which Gill had embraced with energy and courage but with the growing realization that to live there would actually not be possible — a graph of the time that he spent there between 1924 and 1928 would slide pretty steadily downhill all the way. But the romantic pull of the Ewyas valley persisted and two years after he had left Capel Gill purchased the monastery for Betty to open a school. Capel-y-ffin School for Girls (5-15 years of age) was under the patronage of the Lord Bishop of Minevia and boasted a curriculum which included:

> Gardening and dairy work; cooking and all branches of housewifery, including the keeping of household accounts...phonography [shorthand]...spinning and weaving, needlework...music (plain-chant, folk song and dance, violin and pipe)...Elementary Church Latin. etc. (Prospectus 1935).

Visiting staff included "Mr. Eric Gill (Drawing) and Petra Tegetmeier (Spinning and Weaving)" all of which proved so esoteric that the project failed and in 1936 Elizabeth Pepler opened the Monastery as a guest house.

David Jones was deeply affected by the landscape at Capel-y-ffin but it took the rare event of an eclipse of the sun on 29 June 1927 to elicit an aesthetic response to the magnificent environment in the context of Gill's business-like and perfunctory diaries: "The valley in the dim light was strangely beautiful". Gill's work was likewise unresponsive to the actuality of being in Wales; the kinds of things he made could have been produced at Ditchling as they were carried on afterwards at Pigotts. David Jones's work, however, altered under the "impact of the strong hill-rhythms and bright counter-rhythms" of the borderlands. Artistically Jones became, during these years, more supple, individual and mature. Intellectually what Jones carried with him from Ditchling and Capel-y-ffin were rich seeds that would be cultivated by the more urbane intellectual Catholic society in which he participated during the late 1920s, 1930s and early 1940s, and by his own patient and painstaking curiosity that led him to pursue the philosophical problems that he had encountered during his time with Gill. And in Jones's later mythological paintings made after 1940, fragments of received data are subjected to a similar process of eclectic juxtaposition as they are in the later poetry. In works like *The Four Queens* and *Y Cyfarchiad i Fair*, Wales which is seen as an imagined historical, literary and mythological entity is also situated in the actual landscape that Jones remembered from his time in the Ewyas valley.

The beauty of Capel-y-ffin deeply impressed most of the people who lived there or visited. Desmond Chute wrote in a letter of autumn 1928:

> Never shall I forget my visit to the Vale of Ewyas, nor the green light that trickled deliciously into the guest-room, nor the good cheer and the good talk and Betty singing the Sally Gardens (WAC).

Happily today the monastery at Capel-y-ffin is a place where visitors can stay and experience the awesome power of the valley that has attracted people on spiritual pilgrimage for almost a millenium. It is a challenging and uncompromising place, beautiful and tough. David Jones described these 'marches' in 'The Old Quarry' in terms particularly apposite to Eric Gill; he called it a

> place of questioning where you must ask the
> question and the answer questions you' (RQ 18)

— and that is pertinent to all pilgrims.

Bibliography

1. Manuscript and Visual Material

WAC   The bulk of the source material for this book was found among the extensive collection of Gill's diaries, letters and papers in the William Andrews Clark Memorial Library, University of California, Los Angeles.

BM   The British Museum — a collection of Gill's erotica.

GLE   Richard A. Gleeson Library, University of San Francisco — letters and papers of Eric Gill, Philip Hagreen and Desmond Chute.

HRC   Harry Ransom Humanities Research Center, University of Texas, Austin — Transcripts of BBC radio programme on Gill. Also Gill correspondence and visual material.

KYC   Kettle's Yard, Cambridge — David Jones's letters to H.S. Ede.

NLW   The National Library of Wales — manuscripts and letters of David Jones.

V&A   The Victoria & Albert Museum, London — Engravings of Eric Gill.

2. Books and articles consulted – arranged according to abrreviated text references

ACOMC   Herbert Read, 'Eric Gill' in *A Coat of Many Colours* (London, 1945)

AL   Eric Gill, *Art and Love* (Bristol, Douglas Cleverdon, 1927)

AN   Eric Gill, *Art Nonsense and Other Essays*

(London: Cassell, 1929)

ANA — David Jones, *The Anathemata* (London: Faber & Faber, 1952)

AP — Eric Gill, *Art and Prudence* (Waltham St Lawrence: Golden Cockerel Press, 1928)

ARTW — *Artwork* (London, 1930) No 23

AS — Eric Gill, *Architecture and Sculpture* (Royal Manchester Institution, 1927)

AUT — Eric Gill, *Autobiography* (London: Jonathan Cape, 1940)

BBCHRC — Transcripts of 1961 BBC 3rd Programme Broadcast on Eric Gill produced by Douglas Cleverdon

BBCHRCRH René Hague speaking in the above

BCT — David Jones, recorded tape to accompany a British Council Slide Programme edited by Peter Orr

BLAH — Eric Gill, *Beauty Looks After Herself* (London: Sheed and Ward, 1933)

BW WAC — Beatrice Warde, 'Eric Gill, Typographer' — Papers read at a Clark Library Symposium, 22 April 1967

CA — Eric Gill, *Christianity and Art* (Francis Walterson, Abergavenny, 1927)

CG/DK WAC — Cecil Gill interview with David Kindersley at WAC 20 April 1967

CGL — Donald Attwater, *A Cell of Good Living* (London: Geoffrey Chapman, 1969)

CIAP — Jacques Maritain, *Creative Intuition in Art and Poetry* (Princeton, N.J.: Princeton Univ. Press, 1953)

CON — Conversation between Petra Tegetmeier, Derek Shiel and the author, 1989

COPA — Ananda K. Coomaraswamy, *Christian and Oriental Philosophy of Art* (N.Y.: Dover Publications, 1956)

D — Eric Gill, Diaries in WAC

DAP — Dominican Archive, Prinknash

DC DJE — Douglas Cleverdon, *The Engravings of David Jones* (London: Clover Hill Editions, 1981)

DC EEG — *Douglas Cleverdon, The Engravings of Eric Gill* (Wellingborough: Skelton, 1983)

DG — David Jones, *Dai Greatcoat: A Self-Portrait of David Jones in His Letters* ed. René Hague (London: Faber & Fabef, 1980)

DHLP — D.H. Lawrence, 'Art Nonsense and Other Essays by

BIBLIOGRAPHY

	Eric Gill in *Phoenix — The Posthumous Papers of D.H. Lawrence* (London: Heinemann, 1936)
DJ BBC HRC	David Jones in the transcript of the 1961 BBC 3rd Programme broadcast on Eric Gill produced by Douglas Cleverdon.
DJL	David Jones, 'Life for H.S. Ede' — KYC
DK WAC	David Kindersley in the WAC 1967 symposium
DYG	David Jones, *The Dying Gaul and Other Writings* ed. Grisewood (London: Faber & Faber, 1978)
E&A	David Jones, *Epoch & Artist* (London: Faber & Faber, 1959, pbk 1973)
EC	*Herbert Marcuse, Eros and Civilisation* (London: RKP, 1956, pbk 1987)
EEG	1929 *Engravings of Eric Gill* (Bristol: Cleverdon, 1929)
EGMWLL	Roy Brewer, *Eric Gill the Man who Loved Letters* (London: Frederick Muller Ltd., 1973)
EG WAC	Elizabeth Gill, letters in WAC
EPL	Ezra Pound, *Selected Letters 1907–41* ed D.D. Paige (London: Faber & Faber, 1950)
ESS	Eric Gill, *Essays* (London: Jonathan Cape, 1947)
FA	Rayner Heppenstall, *Four Absentees* (London: Barrie & Rockliff, 1960)
FL	*The Fleuron* A Journal of Typography, ed. Morison (Cambridge: C.U.P.)
FN	Eric Gill, *First Nudes* (London, 1954)
FS	Eric Gill, *The Future of Sculpture* (1927) (London: Monotype Corp., 1928)
FVY	Arthur Howell, *Frances Hodgkins: Four Vital Years* (London, 1952)
GKW	*G.K.'s Weekly* (London, 1925–27)
HWE	Albert Garrett, *A History of Wood Engraving* (London: Godfrey Cave, 1986 — Orig. Midas Books, 1978)
IP	David Jones, *In Parenthesis* (London: Faber & Faber, 1937, paperback 1963)
IQ	Eric Gill, *Id Quod Visum Placet* (Waltham St Lawrence, Golden Cockerel Press, 1926)
ISL	Eric Gill, *In a Strange Land* (London, 1944)
JDTR	John Dreyfus, 'Eric Gill's Method of Type Design and Book Illustration' *The Record*, (Univ. of San Francisco No 9, 1972)

BIBLIOGRAPHY

JGLEG	Joanna Gill letters to Eric Gill
JGLEMG	Joanna Gill letters to Eric and Mary Gill
JM	Jonathan Miles, *Backgrounds to David Jones* (Cardiff: Univ. of Wales Press, 1990)
JRMEP	I-M John Rothenstein, *Modern English Painters I-M* (London: Eyre & Spottiswoode, 1956)
JRSL	John Rothenstein, *Summer's Lease* (London, 1965)
JW	Gerald of Wales, *The Journey Through Wales* trans. Lewis Thorpe (Harmondsworth: Penguin, 1978)
LC	William Blissett, *The Long Conversation* (Oxford: O.U.P., 1981)
LE	Eric Gill, *Last Essays* (London: Jonathan Cape, 1942)
LET	Eric Gill, *Letters of Eric Gill* ed. Walter Shewring (London: Jonathan Cape, 1947)
LM	*The London Mercury* Nov. 1931 Vol. XXV No. 145
LMG	Letters of Mary Gill WAC
LSL NLW	David Jones, letters to Saunders Lewis in NLW
MAB GUEST	The Mabinogion trans. by Lady Charlotte Guest (London: Dent, 1906)
MAC	Fiona MacCarthy, *Eric Gill* (London: Faber & Faber, 1989)
MBEG	Cecil Gill, 'My Brother, Eric Gill' (1949)
MG 7&5SC	Mark Glazebrook, *The Seven and Five Society* (London: Michael Parkin Fine Arts, 1979)
MON	Eric Gill, 'The Enormities of Religious Art' in *The Month* January, 1928. A paper read before the Wiseman Society on 17 October 1927
MR	*The Monotype Recorder* (London, March 1958)
MW XXIII	William Morris, *Collected Works* Vol. XXIII (London: Longman's Green & Co, 1914 & 1915)
MY	Malcolm Yorke, *Eric Gill: Man of Flesh and Spirit* (London: Constable, 1981)
NLW 1978 DEP	Deposit of Papers in the NLW by the Executors of David Jones's Estate
ODP	Christopher John Wright, *A Guide to Offa's Dyke Path* (London: Constable, 1975)
OF	*Orate Fratres* (St Paul, Minn., 1927)
OS DW	Oswald Spengler, *The Decline of the West Vols. 1 & 2* trans. Charles Francis Atkinson (London: Allen & Unwi, 1932)
PA	Jacques Maritain, *The Philosophy of Art* trans.

O'Connor (Ditchling, Sussex: St Dominic's Press, 1923)

PAYM James Joyce, *A Portrait of the Artist as a Young Man* (London: Jonathan Cape, 1968)

RCEGAD Richard Cork, Introduction to *Eric Gill — Centenary Exhibition* (London: Anthony D'Offay, 1982)

REG John Rothenstein, *Eric Gill* (London: Ernest Benn, 1927)

RG BC22 Robert Gibbings, 'Memories of Eric Gill' in *The Book Collector* Vol.2 No.2, 1953

RG CDW Robert Gibbings, *Coming Down the Wye* (London: Dent, 1942)

RHDJ René Hague, *David Jones* (Cardiff: Univ. of Wales Press, 1975)

RH LF Robert Harling, *The Letter Forms of Eric Gill* (Svensson, 1976)

RIR Jessie L Weston, *From Ritual to Romance* (1920 — N.Y.: Doubleday, 1957)

RQ David Jones, *The Roman Quarry and Other Sequences* ed. Harman Grisewood & René Hague (London: Agenda Editions, 1981)

RR Peter Anson, *A Roving Recluse* (Cork: Mercier Press, 1946)

RT Jacques Maritain, *Redeeming the Time* trans. Harry Lorin Binsse (London: Geoffrey Bles, The Centenary Press, 1943)

SL David Jones, *The Sleeping Lord* (London: Faber & Faber, 1974)

SM&EG BC Douglas Cleverdon: 'Stanley Morison and Eric Gill'
321 in *The Book Collector* Vol.32 No.1, 1983

SPE Robert Speaight, *The Life of Eric Gill* (London: Methuen, 1966)

TFN Eric Gill, Twenty Five Nudes (1938)

TG Paul Hills, *David Jones* Tate Gallery Catalogue (London: 1981)

TLS *Times Literary Supplement*

WA Eric Gill, 'Intaglio Printing for Woodcuts' in *The Woodcut Annual* No.1 (London: 1927)

WE Ralph John Beedham, *Wood Engraving* (Ditchling, Sussex: St Dominic's Press, 1921)

WP Eric Gill, *Work and Property* (London: Dent, 1937)

3. Books consulted but not cited iby abbreviation n the text

Aquinas, St, Thomas: *Summa Theologica* trans. Fathers of English Dominican Province (N.Y.: Benzinger Bros., 1947–8)
Blackfriars (London: 1925–7)
Bushell, Rev. William Done: *Caldey, An Island of the Saints* (Norwich, 1980)
Clay, Enid: *Sonnets and Verses* (Waltham St Lawrence, Golden Cockerel Press, 1925)
Craig, Gordon: *Hamlet* (Cranach Press, 1930)
Dublin Review, The (1928)
Gibbings, Robert: *12 Wood Engravings* (London, 1921)
Gill, Evan: *Bibliography of Eric Gill* (London: Cassell, 1953)
Gill, Evan: *The Inscription Work of Eric Gill* (London: Cassell, 1964)
Griffith, Wyn: *The Welsh* (Harmondsworth: Penguin, 1950)
Humphreys, Emyr: *The Taliesin Tradition* (London: Black Raven Press, 1983, paperback 1989)
Jones, David: Questionaire in *Wales* (Cardiff, 1946) No. 22
Nash, Paul: *The Book of Genesis* (A.V.) (Nonesuch Press, 1924)
Order, An occasional Catholic Review Nos. 1–4 (London: Bumpus 1928-9)
Pax, Quarterly Review of the Benedictine Monks on Caldey 1925–8
Pepler, Hilary: *A Letter About Eric Gill* (Chicago Ill.: Cherryburn Press, 1950)
Shepherd, Alan: *A Visitor's Guide to Caldey Island* (Cardiff: n.d.)
Williams, Gwyn A: *The Welsh in their History* (London: Croom Helm, 1982)

Acknowledgements

My greatest debt is to Derek Shiel who has generously shared his opinions and insights on the subject of David Jones's paintings and engravings. I would also like to thank Monique Louveau for her kind hospitality which made possible the writing of the book; Catherine Louveau whose support has been constant and considerate; John and Claire Rickard for their help in enabling me to visit obscure parts of the border country and other kindnesses; M. Poeydomenge in Salies-de-Béarn for information about his beautiful town; Mrs Knill at The Monastery, Capel-y-ffin; John Bidwell, Suzanne Wellman and the staff at the William Andrews Clark Memorial Library at UCLA for their attentiveness during the month that I spent with them; also to the staff of the Gleeson Library, University of San Francisco; the staff of the Harry Ransom Humanities Research Center, University of Texas, Austin; the staff of The Tate Gallery Archive; the staff of The National Library of Wales, Aberystwyth; the staff of the Victoria and Albert Museum; the staff of The British Museum Dept. of Prints and Drawings; the staff of the Austin desmond Gallery, London; and the staff of the Anthony D'offay Gallery, London. I should also like to thank Mrs Petra Tegetmeier, Mr & Mrs Tony Hyne, and Mrs Nest Cleverdon and her son Francis for their help.

For financial aid I should like to thank The British Academy for a travel grant, The Henry Moore Foundation for a grant to help with research in the USA and The William Andrews Clark Memorial Library, UCLA for a short-term Residential Fellowship that enabled me to study their extensive Gill collection.

For permission to quote from and reproduce the works of David Jones I should like to thank the Trustees of David Jones's Estate. For permission to quote from and reproduce the works of Eric Gill I should like to thank the Trustees of Eric Gill's Estate.

Publishers' Acknowledgements

Acknowledgement is due to the Estate of David Jones and to Faber & Faber Ltd for permission to quote from *In Parenthesis*, first published in 1937.